Down among the Donkeys

Elisabeth Svendsen MBE

Down among the Donkeys

Pan Original
Pan Books London and Sydney

First published 1981 by Pan Books Ltd,
Cavaye Place, London SW10 9PG
© Elisabeth D. Svendsen 1981
ISBN 0 330 26316 1
Printed and bound by
Hunt Barnard Printing Ltd, Aylesbury, Bucks

to Niels – who else?

Contents

Acknowledgements

My thanks go to many people who throughout my life have helped me do the work to which I am now so deeply devoted; some do deserve special mention, however. I would like my special thanks to go first, of course, to Niels, whose support and fortitude have been invaluable. Then to Lise, Paul, Clive and Sarah, my children, who have had to live with the donkeys. And I would like to thank my sister, Pat Feather, who has always supported me in the past and is now an invaluable help running the Slade Centre for me.

To the trustees of all the charities whose help and advice have always been so willingly given: in particular June Evers, who, living on sanctuary premises, is a constant help and who cheerfully turns out day or night whenever needed; to Rosalind de Wesselow whose donkey expertise has been of the greatest value; and to John Lovell, our lawyer, who is so deeply involved that he is almost one of our staff.

To Julie Courtney, my right hand, I owe a debt of gratitude. She is now my assistant administrator and I value her most highly. Also to Herb and John Fry, such loyal workers for the charity, and each and every one of my thirty staff whose help is so appreciated:

Mr D. Battison, Miss F. Benfield, Mrs M. Bradley,
Miss C. Browning, Mrs D. Charles-Davies, Mr C. Courtney,
Mrs C. Courtney, Mrs J. Courtney, Miss J. Evans,
Mrs P. Feather, Mr R. Forbes, Mr S. Ford, Mr H. Fry,
Mrs J. Fry, Mrs M. Fry, Mr R. Harrington, Mrs S. Harrington,
Mr P. Hartnell, Mrs E. Judge, Mr K. Kiddle, Mr D. Lee,
Mr T. Lee, Miss A. Loosemore, Mr R. Nichols, Mrs E. Payne,
Mr S. Payne, Miss J. Peterken, Mr J. Rabjohns,
Mrs V. Sandon-Humphries, Mrs D. Smith,
Mr S. Thomson, Mr A. Trawford, Mr A. Wardle,
Miss C. Weaver, Mr J. Whitmee.

In particular, I would like to thank Eileen Judge, who spent hours of her own time typing this manuscript.

I would also like to acknowledge help from the following people: Douglas Allen (photographer), Donald Attenburrow and Bob Barker (veterinary surgeons), Ken Birks (advertising agent), Ken Bissel (Sidmouth Printing Works), Ronald Busby (photographer), Eve Bygrave, Bob Camac, Richard Carpenter, Col Gerald Critchley, Brian Drury, Judith Forbes, Susan Greenway (DBS), Mr Holman, Miss Jarrett, Peter Lacey, Mike Northen (DBS), the *Sidmouth Herald*, Tony Scrivens (photographer), and Nicholas Toyne (photographer).

And a very special thank-you to all the people from every part of this country without whose financial support I could not continue to do the work I love.

The author and publishers wish to thank the following for kind permission to reproduce photographs: Douglas Allen, the *Daily Mirror*, Nicholas Toyne.

1 Why donkeys?

Why donkeys? I must be asked this by almost everyone I meet and even now I can't really give them a straightforward answer. It seems that circumstances throughout my life must have led me to the position of being responsible for over seven hundred donkeys and to devoting the major part of my life to these beautiful, gentle, pathetic, mistreated creatures.

My car caught fire! It was early in March 1954, a rainy wet Saturday afternoon. My current boyfriend, Tony, had persuaded me to go to a football match at Halifax and I went because I could try out the new car just provided for me by my father's company for whom I was working. Out we backed on to the main road outside the house and off down the road. Only a short way on the very strong smell of burning became overpowering. I pulled the car to the side of the road, and by the time I had switched off the engine, flames were already coming out of the bonnet and smoke filled the car. I was horrorstruck as it was my new car; I felt quite unable to do anything. Tony was overcome by smoke, retching at the side of the road.

A very old Austin Ruby came chugging up the road towards me. It stopped with a squeal of brakes and out climbed the most handsome man I had ever seen in my life. He grabbed a fire extinguisher from the back of his car, wrenched open the bonnet of my car and within a few seconds all that was left was a horrible smell of burning and a few whiffs of smoke.

'Whatever happened?' asked the strange man, looking me straight in the eye.

'I just don't know,' I answered. 'I'd only just started when this happened. It must have been an electrical fault or something.'

We stood looking at each other across the smouldering bonnet and it is no exaggeration to say that we both fell in love at that moment.

'Do you want any more help?' the tall man asked.

'No, thank you,' I replied weakly, and he turned and got into his car and drove away up the road. I stood mesmerized and watched as he drove into the driveway of a house on the right, almost at the top of the road.

Tony was somewhat irritable for the rest of the day and we spent endless time arranging for the garage to collect the car and for the repairs to be done. I was absentminded as far as Tony was concerned, in fact totally immersed in thoughts about the man who had helped me. It took me three days of cold canvassing up and down Hullen Edge Road with the excuse of looking for a garage for my new car before I met the tall stranger again, but, having met, Niels and I saw each other every single day until our marriage seven months later. The only reason we delayed so long was that Niels was already engaged to a girl in Denmark, and as his total finances were invested in the engagement ring he had sent her we had to wait for it to come back so that he had sufficient money to buy the wedding ring. And also I had to disentangle myself.

I had always been a very skinny, unattractive child, but I managed to have an extremely happy childhood. I was lucky in having an elder sister, Pat, who was an extremely good friend, and kind, fun-loving parents, and we lived in a very old large house called Ashgrove which stood in the industrial part of the West Riding of Yorkshire between Elland and Brighouse. My father worked at the large pipeworks where we mined clay and manufactured drain pipes. This had been founded by my grandfather, who had run it with his two sons.

Up the hill at Ashgrove Cottage lived my father's brother, Stanley, and his three boys, Malcolm, Derek and Brian, and together the five of us really made up a gang who had the most wonderful time, particularly when we went off for day expeditions through the woods and down to the river where we conceived tremendous projects such as building boat-houses, making camps, and even a meeting room which was later, during the war, to be taken over by the fire brigade as their headquarters in our area!

My grandmother suffered badly from asthma and would sometimes go and stay in St Annes for six weeks at a time as the air there suited her. My grandfather visited her every weekend. As my other grandmother lived near Preston, we found ourselves making for Lancashire almost every third weekend. It was always a bit tedious, as we had to be on our best behaviour and it took the whole of a precious Sunday.

One day on the route to St Annes, in my father's little Hillman, which I remember so well, he deviated from his normal route and we went past a field in the Calder Valley. I saw there two donkeys, which thrilled me, and from that day every single weekend we went to Lancashire my father had to go an extra eight miles so that 'little Betty' could see her donkeys. This is the earliest time I remember seeing donkeys and they made an immense impression on me. My father would park as near to the field as he could and I would run across the verge and climb up the post and rail fencing and shout, 'Donkeys!' They would always come right across to me. I think it was then that I really fell in love with them; they had such soft warm muzzles, such beautiful trusting eyes, and they seemed to look at me as if perhaps they knew what was going to happen in the future – I like to think they did, anyway. I was always disappointed when my time was up and I had to get back in the car and face the weekend in St Annes.

In 1939 everything changed, I was nine. My parents were in the United States and Canada on business and in fact sitting on Montreal station the day that war was declared. Pat and I were staying in New Longton with our grandmother and we spent many anxious weeks waiting for them to get back. Prior to going to America my mother had started taking swimming lessons with us and could swim the breadth of the pool. My grandmother always remembered me saying, 'Well, at least if they get torpedoed, they will be able to swim back now.'

Things were never the same after that. My sister and I had to change from Princess Mary High School at Halifax to the grammar school at Brighouse because it was nearer for us travelwise; this made me particularly sad. My best friend was June Evers, with whom I had been going to school since the age of five in Halifax and, of course, she had to stay on there. We did, however, keep in touch and used to go out together almost every weekend.

The first time the sirens went we were all absolutely terrified. My father got out the car and we all drove up to the works and, in the pitch dark, climbed up the ladder to the mine shaft and walked through the mines into the central mine that had been designated as an air-raid shelter. People from Elland gradually came to join us, and there we all sat for five hours in the cold dripping darkness, the men frequently walking the three miles back to the face of the mine to see what was going on. Every second my father was away I imagined him being killed by a bomb and I think the first raids when nothing actually happened were probably the worst ones. Unfortunately our house was near the river Calder and the Germans used to use this as a guide when going to Huddersfield, Bradford and Leeds on bombing raids.

One night we did get three bombs within a quarter of a mile and this was the only time the sirens hadn't gone! My mother was washing my hair at the time and it was as if somebody had banged their fist hard on the bottom of the bath as the first one fell. By the time the third one of the stick had fallen my mother had me out in a towel and downstairs. It is amazing how fast one can move when the necessity arises.

Another vivid memory is of a Sunday afternoon when my mother had brought out a long-saved tin of pineapple, a real luxury in those days, and we were just about to have the first mouthful when we heard an aeroplane coming over the house

14

extremely low. We all ran into the garden and saw a small plane at roof height, skimming down towards the river below the house. A few seconds later came the sound of a terrible crash. We ran down through the garden, across the daffodil fields, through the railings that separated us from the canal and the river. There, slowly sinking, was a small single-engined plane with the pilot trapped in the cockpit. I hadn't realized how brave my father was until this moment, but without any hesitation he jumped straight into the water, swam across to the plane and, with my grandfather, who had arrived on the bank, shouting instructions, managed to pull himself up on the sinking wings and push the cockpit roof back. My mother, next to me, was shouting, 'Vincent, do be careful, it's going to blow up.' But he took no notice and within minutes was helping the very dazed pilot out. The plane had ploughed through electric cables as it came in across the field and my father had to help the airman back across the canal rather than risk touching the cables on the aircraft.

The pilot, Wendell Nelson, was an American and became a firm friend of our family, visiting us frequently on his leaves. Sadly, he was shot down over the North Sea two years later. He made a great impression on our family and we still keep in contact with his friend, Bob Wallis, whom he used to bring with him.

I was never a very healthy child. I seemed to get every illness and sickness in the book, and I remember with the greatest pleasure the recuperation times I was given after severe bouts of scarlet fever, chicken pox, measles and whooping cough. I would wander round our wonderful wild garden spending hours watching small wildlife. My mother frequently had to put up with small boxes of injured creatures reviving in the safety of my bedroom. There was the small hedgehog, Benjy, I took in. He lived in my room in a shoebox for about five weeks, recovering, I hoped, from being knocked unconscious on the busy road outside our house. One morning at about five o'clock a strange pattering sound woke me; it sounded like rain on the windows and in fact I looked there first before realizing that the noise came from Benjy's box in the corner. I opened the lid. Benjy the hedgehog had died, and leaping up and down were what can only be described as thousands of insects of varying sizes banging themselves in a futile attempt to escape from the box. I was quite horrified, having no idea that Benjy was host to such a large number of parasites, and for quite a while hedgehogs didn't appear in my bedroom.

It wasn't easy for my parents, living next door to my grandfather and grandmother before they retired to St Annes permanently, particularly when Grandpa ran the works and he would come round during the evening asking Father to go back and stoke up a kiln, or deal with some difficult sales crisis. I wasn't surprised when my parents decided that we should buy a house in Elland itself so that they could have a little more privacy and for the first time their own house.

They fell in love with a house called Windy Ridge situated up Hullen Edge Road in Elland and managed to find the necessary deposit. We all moved in in 1943. I missed the old garden terribly and found the journey to school extremely difficult as I had to walk down 'the steps', as they were known, which consisted of over two hundred steep steps on to a lower road, catch a trolley bus into Elland and then a petrol bus to Brighouse. The return journey was even worse and, having come out of school at four o'clock, I didn't get home until twenty past five. One particular Friday evening I felt ill and remember crawling up the steps at Hullen Edge and struggling to get back to the house, feeling absolutely terrible. My father was fitting curtains that night and I lay in bed wondering when the banging was ever going to stop. The next morning the doctor was called and acute appendicitis diagnosed. The appendix had ruptured by the time they operated but they seemed to think it had been drained sufficiently. After two weeks in hospital I was sent home apparently cured.

I didn't feel it, in fact I felt awful for the next three or four weeks. To cheer me up Dad suggested a family outing to see the music hall star Norman Evans at Halifax Palace; and one Thursday evening we all went by bus to see the performance. Halfway through, whilst Norman Evans was doing his 'Over the garden wall' act, I remember feeling a very sharp pain shooting through my right hand, and looking down in the dim lights of the theatre I could see it looked slightly different from the other. The doctor came the next day and he thought it was a little arthritis, perhaps.

16

Over the next few days, though, not only my hand but my whole arm started swelling and despite sulphonamide treatment and every drug known at that time nothing seemed to slow the infection's pace. When the pain was halfway down my back and I was almost totally delirious I was once again admitted to the Duke of York's Hospital.

I can remember lying in bed and although I was reputedly unconscious I could hear every word that was being said and heard the specialist telling my parents that there was no hope at all, I had something called septicaemea which had turned into osteomyelitis, a disease which ended in death. Although I heard this and saw my parents' tear-stained faces I really wasn't very concerned. In fact I was floating happily above them, held on what appeared to be a very thin thread, and beyond the long corridor that I felt to be in I could see the faces of people who I had loved and who had died and who were all waiting for me. It was the most magnificent feeling of freedom and exhilaration, one quite inexplicable, which has made me confident that there is a life after death and has left me with no fear at all of dying.

I saw myself being wheeled away. I saw myself in the operating theatre and I never felt so disappointed in my life as when I was dragged back to my body on the table. Having been given no hope my parents signed an operating form and agreed to the use of the trial of penicillin which so far, to the best of my knowledge, had only been used on the British army in Bradford. There is no doubt it saved my life.

The next three years were very hard indeed for me, I had so many operations we all lost count. Every time the hand and arm seemed to be settling down another piece of bone would break away and have to be removed and although I managed to return to school after the first year I wasn't allowed out in the playground at lunchtime and had to go for dressings twice a day to the doctor's surgery and for massage three afternoons a week, so I was different from all the other girls. One day the headmistress called my parents to school and said, 'I'm very sorry, Mr Knowles, but Betty won't be able to sit her school certificate as there seems very little chance that she'll pass.'

Now by this time Pat had obtained a place at the Rachel

McMillan Training College, where she was going to become a teacher, and I desperately wanted to follow in her footsteps. The headmistress, Miss Ford, was persuaded to let me take the exams even though not being able to use my right hand made things extremely difficult. I did manage to get my school certificate with seven passes and credits, the most surprising being a credit in art where they seemed to appreciate the peculiar style I had developed with my left hand!

I developed a tremendous faith in life and its purpose and I felt that for some reason I had been spared death and felt determined to find that reason. My parents had always taken us to church regularly and I was confirmed by Thomas Cashmore, then the vicar of Brighouse and one of the greatest friends and advisers I have had in my life. Confirmation meant a great deal to me and the ideals I learned then and through my association with Thomas Cashmore, now retired Bishop of Dunwich, have stood me in good stead for the rest of my life.

My poor parents really had some problems with me! In the sixth form I was sitting quietly studying one day when my friend casually threw a pair of scissors to the girl sitting next to me working on embroidery. The first thing I was aware of was something striking my eye and within twenty minutes we were once again on our way to Bradford but this time to the eye infirmary. For three weeks both eyes were bandaged and serious permanent injury averted. Once again I was given time to sit and think and work things out; at the age of seventeen it made a deep and lasting impression upon me. I found I seemed to know when people were coming and to be able to feel their thoughts very much more than when I was busy on my normal teenage occupations which had always seemed so important.

College was a very happy time for me. The buildings were situated in the heart of the slums of London, in Deptford. The college provided a very real chance to work with deprived children and to learn a great deal of psychology, philosophy and teaching. It was nice to come out with a first-class Froebel certificate to start me on my teaching career.

I decided to live at home as Pat had by this time married and moved away. I settled in at Windy Ridge and got a job at the local school at West Vale. Bearing in mind that I had just finished three years' training the main emphasis of which was using the full facilities of the school, in particular for creative play, I took my nursery class into the little garden every day and set up easels, waterplay, sand and so on which the children used to the fullest possible creative advantage. The visiting inspector to the school was absolutely appalled and I was summoned to the headmaster's office and told by the inspector that unless I brought the children indoors and taught them properly, sitting at tables, I would get a letter from the local authority. In the end I decided to carry on teaching as I had been trained. Once again, by pure coincidence, the same inspector arrived and I received a very severe dressing-down.

My father's company was progressing well and the secretary, Fanny Sutcliffe, who had been there since my grandfather founded it thirty-two years before, was the mainstay of the office. Then, suddenly, Fanny suffered a stroke and it seemed she would not be able to work for some months, if ever. Realizing I was unhappy, my father asked me to give up teaching and help run the works. It seemed the right psychological moment to make a change. I learned touch-typing, shorthand and book-keeping at night school and served my notice as a teacher.

It was certainly different working in an office tackling large wage sheets for over a hundred men, twenty-eight of whom were miners and had different shift rates and bonuses, and the rest of whom were piece-workers and every single person paid at a different rate! I got through and the men got wages. Those that didn't get enough complained, and those that got too much never said anything, so eventually it all worked out. The selling side of the business on which my father concentrated interested me and I began doing the selling for him over the telephone.

I had learned to drive at college but until one particular Saturday morning I hadn't driven anything larger than my father's car. On this Saturday I was alone in the office when a very irate customer from an airfield near Hull rang complaining that the load of pipes promised the day before hadn't been delivered; his men were working overtime at the weekend and what were we going to do about it? I found our driver had been taken ill and it had been assumed that the load could go on the Monday. Our very good customer didn't agree, so I said, 'Well, never mind, we'll get it there somehow.' My father and his brother Stanley were away so I decided to take this six-ton load myself. In those days gears weren't quite so easy as today and double declutching was essential. It took three telephone books propped in the back of the seat before I could even push in the clutch pedal completely and when I left the yard with all the pipes juddering round my ears in the cab behind me I did hope I was doing the right thing! It seemed hundreds of miles but in fact was just about sixty to Hull.

Every traffic light was a challenge and every hill a nightmare. There was a whole row of men who were busy digging a trench where the pipes were to be laid, and as I drew up not a head moved. Suddenly as I opened the door and began the jump down one of the men saw me and a stunned silence fell upon the line of men as I climbed down from the wagon and said, 'Well, who's going to help me unload, then?' After that I always got a lot more respect from the men in our yard when I walked in.

I seemed to have a whole horde of boyfriends, none particularly serious. I like men to be companions and that was the main ingredient for a good boyfriend. My parents got a little confused with so many boys phoning and calling at the house, and my father put a list by the telephone and I had to put what division I classed them in, i.e. first, second or third division. If a third-divisioner rang up my father would say happily, 'Oh no, I am sorry she's busy tonight,' and only first-divisioners got priority. He could not understand that Niels Svendsen walked away with the cup without even appearing in the divisions!

Niels, despite his name, is British and his family had come to England years before. His mother had married twice and he had six brothers and half-brothers. He was born in 1929 and brought up mainly in a large house on the outskirts of Exeter by his step-father, Svend Iversen. He was always very mechanically minded and at the age of seventeen purchased a very old motor-bike, which he took apart, reconstructed and sold at a good profit. His business acumen developed early!

Niels did his national service in the RAF, working on radar and eventually going to Malta; he had an accident there which affected his left eye permanently, and he was invalided out of the RAF and went back to Exeter. Niels had already been accepted to read chemistry at Exeter University and added botany, having done some work in that field between leaving the RAF and going up. His grant was only two pounds a week and things were very tough for a while, but he supplemented the grant with extra money made from photography.

At the end of the third year, having obtained his BSc, he won a scholarship to Cambridge to study tropical agriculture, which would lead to a job in Trinidad. During the summer holidays, however, one of his elder brothers, Jørgen, offered him a job in the new business he had started at Elland in Yorkshire. Niels became so involved in the manufacture of Metalife, a liquid zinc-rich paint that stopped rust, that he was persuaded by his brother to stay on after the time he should have gone to Trinidad; and he managed to obtain a year's extension on that grant.

Niels lived with Jørgen and his wife on Hullen Edge Road, in fact about eight houses above Windy Ridge, and it was whilst driving back from work on Saturday that he came across the car in the road that had contained me! Niels could do everything better than I could. It really was the first time that I ever seemed to have met somebody who I could respect in every way.

When Niels had an argument with his brother and moved to a flat in a very old house on the outskirts of Halifax, we would sit evening after evening listening to classical records, reading philosophers like Ouspensky, talking and exploring each other's minds into the long hours of the night. In these permissive days I suppose some people may find it hard to believe that at this stage sex never came into our meetings apart from the inevitable kiss and cuddle but this was something that we were saving till we were married.

It gave us time to really get to know each other and to become the tremendous companions which we still are today. We played tennis in the snow at the end of March, we played golf, we swam, we fished, and we worked together. Many a weekend we spent painting chimneys with Metalife in that area and many a large vault in Yorkshire wool mills has been personally painted by Niels and me!

One game of golf was to have far-reaching consequences. There was a terrible hole at Bradley Hall Golf Club where we played – the thirteenth! You had to drive over a deep ravine to reach the green and Niels' ball always landed in the stream which ran down it. The first time he ever did a perfect drive and got across, he turned to me flushed with elation and said, 'Darling, will you marry me?' And I said, 'Yes!'

My parents loved Niels from the minute they met him and he fitted into our family in a most amazing way. The only thing my father never got used to was his surname; he would have preferred a good old Yorkshire name in the family. We converted a flat at Ashgrove and after our marriage on 20 October 1954 moved into a flat in the house in which I was born.

I thought I had known a great deal about Niels before we got married but I had no idea of his inventive genius until I found that the new cooker, a wedding present from my parents, could be used to wake us up in bed. Niels, having sent me out on a long shopping expedition, completely rewired it to the bedroom radio and the automatic setting on the electric oven blasted us out of bed at seven o'clock on a regular basis. It was a bit difficult to accept that when I switched on the grill I was more likely to get 'Music whilst I worked' than toast!

We were pretty hard up and had very little money with which to furnish our rented flat, which ran the full length of the old converted stable. Our bedroom was at one end and Niels had the rather strange habit of coming to bed at night by setting off from the kitchen at ninety miles an hour, running down the corridor and then leaping on to the bed. One thing we had invested in was a good double bed!

By June, to our horror, we found the bed collapsing on us and I rang the manufacturers, who had specifically quoted how strong and durable it was. Their representative came round to have a look and he and I removed the mattress and stood gazing at the metal base. The whole frame was bent in the middle and this of course made the mattress sag. He looked at me with a horrified expression on his face and said, 'What on earth's been happening to the bed?' As his eyes gazed at mine he suddenly became aware that I was six months pregnant, and a slow blush began to appear over his face. 'I, I do beg your pardon,' he stammered. 'Of course we will refund the money for the bed.' And the next day we received a cheque for the full amount in the post.

Lise was born safely, albeit three weeks late, on 13 October. The doctor had booked me into the nursing home three days previously and I had suffered all sorts of indignities as they tried to get my daughter to make her appearance in the world. Having failed my third medical induction the night before she was born, I was absolutely fed up when Niels came to visit me.

Niels has never been good at hospital visiting and he sat by my bed very miserably. 'I really wanted to go and see *The Dambusters* in Huddersfield.' 'So do I,' said I, sitting bolt upright in bed. 'Let's go,' I got dressed quickly and quietly and left a note on the pillow saying, 'Gone to the pictures, back later.' We crept away into the night. There was a long queue when we got to the cinema but the manager took pity on us and my obvious state, and the usherette when moving us along the row flashed her torch into people's faces and said, 'Stand *well* back, please, ladies and gentlemen,' and so I managed to totter to a seat. The labour pains started halfway through the film but we were determined to see the end. A very angry nursing staff, who weren't used to their patients opting out on them, met us when we got back but they were pleased that the sortie seemed to have set things going; by lunchtime the next day Lise had arrived.

Seven days later was our first wedding anniversary. I asked my mother if she would bring my wedding dress in to the hospital so I could meet Niels with it on, holding the baby – my idea of a joke. Of course when it arrived I couldn't fit into it as my 22-inch waist had changed somewhat drastically. My mother provided me with a white nightdress and it never ceases to surprise me that Niels' first comment was 'Darling, how did you manage to get into your wedding dress?' A Marks & Spencer's nightie would have done just as well as a wedding dress so far as Niels was concerned!

Lise was a great joy, but it was a difficult period for us as Niels and his brother unfortunately fell out over the share structure of their new company and this meant Niels looking for a new job. So with our small baby, Lise, we left home and the North and moved to Bridgwater in Somerset, where he became a manager at British Cellophane.

For me the move meant losing my job at the works. Even though I had Lise and another baby on the way I did feel that there had to be more to life than a constant round of nappies. Niels and I were both twenty-six, full of energy and enthusiasm, and we gradually realized there was no quick way to the top through Niels' present job. We talked and talked and talked and finally decided to form our own company. To do what? We still had to decide.

The seemingly endless rows of wet nappies provided the answer; a simple, efficient dryer was what was urgently needed and we decided this was the product we would design, manufacture and sell.

We found a 'lazy tong' rack in Woolworths and Niels wound an electric element into a biscuit tin. We filled the rack with wet nappies and placed it over the biscuit tin. Niels plugged in his new invention and we stood back to see how quickly the nappies would dry.

'It's working,' I said, happily, as clouds of steam began to appear from the nappies, and then we smelt it! It was not steam emerging but smoke from our scorching carpet! We realized that to achieve convection currents the heater would have to be lifted off the floor; the next attempt with legs worked, but the strange black square on the carpet remained with us for life. Once Niels had perfected the dryer we chose the name Modern Equipment Company and set up our small partnership. The total capital we could scrape together was £120 and with this and unlimited enthusiasm we started. Niels was being paid £800 a year and apart from buying the normal essentials of life I had to budget for thermostats, elements, wooden racks and sales leaflets. We had to order 200 cases before the Bridgwater firm would accept an order from us and we had to store these in our bathroom as it was the only space we had! Niels rushed home every evening from work, straight into the little potting shed we rented and assembled dryers from the parts we had purchased. I would set off in our small van with Lise and my bump to do my best to sell them.

Trying to get a firm in Bristol to buy some dryers, and not feeling particularly well, I sat down in the shop and the buyer asked me rather anxiously when the baby was due. I explained it was already three weeks late; in a panic he immediately signed the order with no further dispute. I left happily. Selling while extremely pregnant was very beneficial to our company!

We took on a nurse this time as I had hated hospitals and she moved in the day Paul was due. It was quite a squeeze on our resources having to pay the nurse and feed her whilst waiting for Paul to make his appearance. The nurse was a very keen knitter and had set up her machine in our lounge; it had driven us mad for the last three weeks and when I got my first pains I quietly retreated into our bedroom next door as much to get away from the noise of the knitting machine as to have the baby! The 1957 Oxford and Cambridge Boat Race was on and Niels was happily watching it with roars of 'in, out, in, out' coming from the box. The whole thing happened so quickly that nobody heard my first two or three shouts. By the time Niels and the nurse arrived Paul was already halfway into the world. He was a super baby, with a very placid character, and he and Lise, who adored him from the moment he arrived, were wonderful children.

By January 1958 we had got the dryers into places like Harrods and Heals of London but desperately needed more capital. Some good friends in Bridgwater bravely volunteered and our little company then became a limited concern. One of the new shareholders drew our attention to an advertisement in the *News Chronicle*, offering a prize for the person most able to 'get ahead' in a business if they were given a prize of £5,000. This was to be televised over a twelve-week period and we decided to apply. We wrote a long letter putting forward our reasons why we thought we were most able to get ahead and to our joy the application was selected for the final. It was exciting just being invited up to London by the *News Chronicle*. We stayed at the Clarendon Court Hotel up the Edgware Road and the television programmes came from the Maida Vale studio only two miles away.

The judges were Lady Lewisham, Lord Halsbury, Sir Frederick Hooper and George Woodcock. On the day of the actual programme we were incredibly nervous. Each contestant had somebody to look after him and we thought how kind of the BBC until Niels realized that the Mr Pickwick assigned to him wasn't doing it for Niels' sake but to make quite sure he didn't slip off and miss the programme. It was an absolutely nail-biting experience but to our amazement and delight Niels came up with the right answers and won the treasured prize of £5,000.

Niels went back to work when we got home next morning but after two hours I had to telephone him to come back home quickly and help. A constant stream of visitors arrived wanting to buy the dryers, people telephoned to offer advice, or for jobs and journalists to interview us. Niels had to pack in his job with British Cellophane and come in full time as managing director of the Modern Equipment Company Ltd. We had planned a very elaborate campaign to get ahead with the £5,000, because although the sum was large enough to solve our immediate financial problems it had to be doled out very carefully if we were to expand the business as fully as we wanted.

We invested in a typist, which relieved a lot of my time from some of the more mundane tasks of writing letters and making out invoices. The progress of our company was quite meteoric. I was in charge of the sales side and Niels of the manufacturing side, and by 1960 we eventually had to build our own factory in Yeovil. Building up the business so rapidly involved an enormous amount of work and both Niels and I learned all the way. A year later we had three sorts of dryers on the market and a turnover approaching half a million pounds.

Up to now we had always rented flats and houses as all our money was invested firmly in the business. The children were very happy and growing up fast. Niels and I were delighted to find that another baby was on the way in 1961, as we had always wanted at least four children. At this time in West Chinnock, the village where we lived near Yeovil, a building plot became available which we bought and with the help of an extremely good local builder we built Deepwell House. It was a beautiful dream house built of local stone and had two and a half acres of ground.

Once settled in, we bought Donko, our first donkey, who became one of the family from the second he arrived. The children really loved him and we all spent happy hours going on expeditions, playing cowboys and Indians with Donko helping both sides, and otherwise living a contented family life.

As children we had our holidays on the Norfolk Broads and I had always loved sailing. Niels was very enthusiastic to try and living near the sea we decided to buy a small sailing dinghy and try our hand at dinghy racing. We joined Lyme Regis Club. Niels, of course, was skipper and I was the crew and on a 505 one of the skills was that the crew 'trapezes'. You wear a special harness and with the edge of your toes on the gunnels clip on the wire which is attached to the mast and as the boat heels over you project yourself out over the sea as far as possible.

We certainly had some hilarious times, Niels was learning the art of helmsmanship and quite frequently he decided to come about whilst I was still out on the wire. This led to frequent duckings and capsizes and eventually led, I think, to our only real row. Having capsized three times in one particular race Niels pulled me aboard spluttering and indicated that I was not fit to crew his boat! That did it, I did not say a word, I merely went back into the water and swam the mile and a half back to the club house leaving Niels on his own to try and finish the race. By the time a quiet Niels arrived back at the club house I had been through the *Yachts and Yachting* magazine, found a 505 for sale called *Cresta*, telephoned the owner and arranged to see the boat the next day.

Needless to say, I went ahead and bought my own boat and with a super young crew we competed against Niels even to the stage of the national championships in Torquay where I was the only woman helm.

We did have great fun and I think it fair to say that the honours were fairly equal and we were delighted to be awarded the Lyme Regis Sailing Club Sportsman of the Year trophy, mainly, I think, because we swam past the finishing post so many times!

My third pregnancy was highly enjoyable as the business was going very well; as usual the baby was three weeks late and was born at home so that the waiting time didn't interfere with home or business life. In the event the birth turned out to be quite terrifying. Clive was born safely, at just over nine pounds, and everything seemed to be going extremely well, when I began to haemorrhage severely. For a short time it seemed that Clive might be motherless, but a hastily summoned ambulance from Crewkerne, with sirens blazing through the village, arrived in the nick of time and the essential blood transfusion saved the day. Now with three fine healthy children we talked seriously about a fourth. There were many children in need of good homes and the adoption societies were always looking for suitable parents to take these children in. It was never the fair-haired blue-eyed beautiful child who needed the home badly, rather those slightly handicapped in some way, and we resolved there and then that in view of the plight of so many babies, we would adopt our next child.

We were expanding our business faster and faster and Niels was interested in going into the dishwasher market, which we felt was going to be the up-and-coming domestic appliance of the future. Thorn Electrical Industries saw us at the Ideal Home Exhibition in 1961 demonstrating our dishwasher and eventually made such a tempting offer that we were persuaded to sell out and we joined Tricity of Thorn Electric.

Both of us had mixed feelings over the sale of 'Modeq'; we had had such great fun building it up together that we had the usual worries about how to work as small cogs in such a very large organization. Our fears were well founded. The promises made by Thorn in good faith had to be broken as problems struck the domestic appliance market and the manufacture of our dryer was moved to their factory in the North. With the greatest difficulty we found jobs for all our workers, sold our beautiful house and moved up to their London offices.

We settled on Bourne End in a nice house near the river, where the children seemed to thoroughly enjoy themselves falling in and out of canoes on the little Abbotsbrook that flows into the Thames. They were all developing strong personalities by this time and we all made the most of our stay near London with its theatres and galleries and museums. Niels and I joined the Upper

Thames Yacht Club and, our earlier differences settled, competed in the International 14 Class. We really had some fun. On one occasion I remember us sailing triumphantly past the club house, having won a race in a particularly tricky wind. Our spinnaker was up and in full view of the race committee and spectators we broke our concentration with a great hug and kiss and then, before we knew it, we were both catapulting through the air. The spinnaker sheet had caught on one of the mooring posts a few feet off the bank! What a capsize to remember but it was well worth while and we both crawled out muddy and laughing to face the task of sorting our upturned boat out. Sailing the Upper Thames reaches has always been tricky, in places the houses cut off all the wind and on one hot airless day one old lady opened her window as we drifted by and Niels is sure the draught she made enabled us to pass two boats.

Sadly the liaison with Thorn didn't work out as we had all hoped. We did find it very difficult to be employees and eventually packed it in, sold up again and took our little family down to Cornwall to start the demanding job of putting a boatyard back on its feet.

Whilst we did enjoy Cornwall, particularly the sailing and the fact that we had much more time to be with our children, the climate was horrible. The winter mists came in during early November and until March we seemed to sit in a damp humid atmosphere feeling pathetic and sorry for ourselves. We sat for hours thinking what sort of new business we could form; we loved working together and wanted the fun and challenge of starting a new company. Our thoughts turned to hotel life. This seemed an ideal way of being able to live comfortably with one's capital in a safe place and to be able to have sufficient staff around to make a social life somewhat easier with a perpetual supply of baby-sitters!

Parting with Donko had been a real sorrow when we moved from Deepwell and the children were constantly asking for another donkey; it was in the back of my mind that we might find somewhere with enough ground to start a small donkey stud and I was very keen to try my hand at breeding donkeys.

After a search lasting about six months we found the Salston Hotel at Ottery St Mary in Devonshire. This was an extremely large old country house with eight acres of ground, almost completely run down and seemingly ideal for our purposes. We were hooked immediately and the challenge of building it up began.

2 A charity is formed

As we walked into the hotel on a Saturday in March 1966, the staff all walked out! I am sure there was nothing personal in it and we learned later that new owners and previous staff never seem to mix in the hotel world. A dance was booked for the evening. There was a very large bar to man and apparently twenty-five people were coming to have dinner in the restaurant. To say that evening was a shambles would be the most complete understatement. We were lucky that while in Cornwall we had made friends with Mo and Keith who had had a little hotel experience. They came to help initiate us and thank goodness they were there because we rushed madly between kitchen, dining room and bar where over a hundred people gathered and drank enormous quantities of most peculiar drinks which we had to ask about before being able to serve!

Naughty Face arrives outside the Salston Hotel

Most of the clientele appeared to arrive on motor-bikes, and eventually at just after half past twelve Niels went into the ballroom and asked the band to stop playing and close for the evening since fights were breaking out left, right and centre and we felt the situation was getting completely out of control. When finally the last unwilling guest had been physically pushed out of the hotel and the big doors were locked we all sank down in the bar and miserably wondered what on earth we had let ourselves in for.

During the next week we managed to start accumulating some staff, and the next weekend was in fact a little easier, although peppered with small incidents such as the one where our new chef took a carving knife to one of the kitchen hands who was not doing his job well enough. We both felt completely wretched and realized we had made the most terrible mistake assuming firstly that the hotel industry was something one could walk into easily and secondly that one could make a good living from it just like that.

An upstairs room in the hotel over the large ballroom had to be made into a flat with two bedrooms for us and we certainly found it different from the acres of room we'd had in the past. We had not forgotten our pledge to adopt our fourth child and had made one attempt in Cornwall. We thought that Paul, our eldest son, would benefit greatly by going into a small boarding school on the coast near our home to have more individual teaching attention. At the delightful little school he attended was an abandoned baby in the care of the Cornwall health authorities. He seemed desperately in need of a home as his parents were unable to care for him and so we made the necessary applications through the county council. The papers for this child were eventually passed on to the National Children's Adoption Association and Miss Hilary Halpin from there got in touch with us and advised us officially that we could start arrangements for adoption. We were all so excited, he seemed such a dear little boy, and Paul was fond of him already. Lise, our eldest daughter, offered to go to the same school as Paul so she too could get to know Rupert and it would be less traumatic for him when he eventually arrived with us.

After Lise had spent a term at the school we received a notification from the adoption association to say that regretfully the child had been withdrawn from the adoption list and it would no longer be possible for us to consider adoption. We went up to see Miss Halpin and told her that we were quite willing to take in any other child in desperate need, we didn't mind which sex and that we were prepared to take one that could not normally be placed for any particular reason. We filled in forms galore and provided references and we both had to have medical examinations! The paperwork was laborious but we supposed the association was doing its best to make sure we were suitable parents.

On 19 February 1968 we received a telephone call from Miss Halpin to tell us that they had a baby on their books whom they thought was extremely suitable for us. She was a little girl, her parents were not English, and there were certain medical problems which made her unadoptable. They suggested we came up to see the baby and along with the letter came a little form saying: 'We would be glad if you would bring a suitcase with you for any clothes or possessions the baby may have and a shawl. Will you also please bring a carrycot with appropriate cot bedding. The baby will have a tin of food which he/she is having at present, a bottle already made up for the journey and full directions for feeding.'

It was suddenly very exciting to think that we were going to have another daughter and we held an immediate family conference to make sure the children were still as enthusiastic as they had been earlier on. It was really super to see their faces light up in anticipation of the new addition to the family and the fact that the baby would need extra care seemed to make it all even more worth while. It seemed funny packing a carrycot but we put all the baby's needs in it, including the shawl, and received a very excited send-off from the children and the staff at the hotel as we set off to catch the train for London.

We had decided to travel first class so we could look after the baby properly on the way home and got two seats in a compartment already occupied by a businessman and a very elderly couple who could only be described as 'posh'. Niels slung the carrycot on to the luggage rack, left the newspapers on the seat, and we both went up the train to get breakfast. Back in our compartment we found the elderly couple no longer there and the gentleman reading and smiling away in the corner of the compartment. Two minutes later he put down his book and said, 'I really must tell you what happened when you went out.' We were quite surprised as people rarely talk in first-class compartments, but he obviously had a great deal on his mind. 'The moment you went out,' he said, 'the lady started getting at her husband. "Fancy," she said. "Fancy throwing that poor little thing up there on the luggage rack and not even bothering to see if it was all right. Get straight up there, Henry, and have a look at it." "Darling," Henry said, "we really shouldn't interfere. They must know what they are doing." "Henry, you are to get up there straight away and see if that baby is all right. I am not going to sit in this carriage and allow that sort of cruelty to take place." '

Apparently poor Henry stood on tiptoe on the seat but could not see in. 'Lift it down,' the wife had insisted. 'Lift it down and look at it, it might be smothering.' And so they lifted the carrycot down on to the seat, and their surprise to find an empty carrycot was only exceeded by their extreme embarrassment; apparently they had put the cot back and gone to another compartment.

Of course we arrived at the adoption agency far too early for our appointment at three thirty, so we wandered round Harrods. I had never been to their antique department before and was immensely excited by the beautiful things for sale. Suddenly I saw the most beautiful pair of Georgian candlesticks. 'Golly, Niels,' I said, 'those are absolutely fantastic. I wonder how much they are.' Poor Niels, he could see that look in my eyes, and knowing my love of Georgian silver knew what was about to happen. Niels' face was a treat as I signed the cheque, it was one of the biggest we had made out but I knew that it was a really good pair of sticks. 'What with a pair of sticks and a baby it is becoming quite a feat,' said Niels.

At half past three exactly we found ourselves talking to Miss Halpin. 'Your baby is lying on a table in this little room. There is a pair of weighing scales next to the baby and we will leave you alone with her to make your minds up,' she said, opening the door to a room where there was an enormous table and lying in the middle of it, stark naked, was our little Sarah! I don't think either of us could say she was the most beautiful child we had ever seen; she had congenitally dislocated hips which made her tiny form on the table look very strange, she was covered in a rash, her nose was running as she had a slight cold and her eyes were most definitely going in opposite directions! We stood together at the side of the table just looking. She looked at us and her little face was all screwed and puckered up.

'For heaven's sake,' said Niels, 'get some nappies on and put a shawl on and let's get her back home.' And so little Sarah joined our family. The formalities at that stage were almost nil. We signed the adoption association's form and then it was back to the station in a taxi and down to Exeter. Our companion from the morning's journey was waiting on the station and I think he enjoyed as much as we did Sarah having her first bottle on the way home and our obvious joy and enthusiasm at the new addition to the family. We didn't get back until nearly eleven and crept quietly in the front door of the hotel, Niels carrying the cot. There in the lounge were all our friends and children waiting to greet the new little baby. They had all brought gifts for Sarah, and Niels was so overwhelmed he opened two bottles of champagne there and then and we all drank a toast to the latest Svendsen.

The next day our doctor saw Sarah and arranged for her to see an eye specialist immediately as obviously her sight was very impaired and she was going to need a series of operations to restore proper vision. In fact we didn't realize until she started crawling and toddling just how bad it really was. Her little head was always a mass of bruises as she walked into things and we were very lucky to have as good a children's eye specialist as Mr Cantrell from Exeter. The doctor looked at her little congenitally dislocated hips and although he felt she would probably need a plaster cast in the very near future, he decided to sort out the eye problem first and advised massage of her legs every time I changed her nappy. The actual legal adoption officially took place after the many formalities, including court medicals for ourselves and the baby, on 17 June 1968, and on Thursday 20 June, Niels' birthday, we were able to announce in the births column of the

Daily Telegraph: 'Svendsen (adoption) by Betty (*née* Knowles) and Niels Svendsen of the Salston Hotel, Ottery St Mary, a daughter Sarah Anna, a sister for Lise, Paul and Clive.'

It was lovely being able to look after the baby on my own. There had always been my work with Lise, Paul and Clive, but having the hotel meant working from home rather than having to go to an office. We took on a lovely girl called Sue Rist, whose sister had been working in the hotel since we bought it, to be Sarah's nanny, and also resident nanny to all the children who arrived at the hotel. She was extremely good with Sarah and the other children and as the hotel got busier it was essential that she was there all the time.

It was August 1969 when donkeys really began to come into my life in a big way. We had all missed Donko since we left West Chinnock and while idly looking through the pages of the *Exeter Express & Echo*, the local paper, my eyes suddenly became riveted on one small advertisement. 'Livestock for Sale' was the heading: 'Pedigree donkey mare for sale, Kennetbury Martha. Apply Mr Mogar.' It had an Ottery St Mary telephone number. Niels was unable to resist my pleadings to ring up immediately and as a result a few minutes later we jumped into the car with all the children and drove up to West Hill where we met Naughty Face, officially known as Kennetbury Martha, for the very first time. She had such beautiful limpid eyes and such an intelligent face that I really have to blame her for everything that happened after.

She cost £45 and Cdr Mogar promised to deliver her when a stable had been built and a fence erected around the field in front of the Salston Hotel. I bought three bales of straw to make her a nice deep bed.

Niels, with the help of Keith, our friend from Cornwall, and Herb Fry, the gardener, got the work done and one week later Naughty Face arrived. Down the ramp of the wagon she walked, looked at Niels and me calmly, and then trotted off to inspect her field and shelter. I stood by the rails absolutely entranced by the way she moved, the intelligence used in examining her new surroundings and the way that every few moments she would come back to me at the fence to gently nuzzle my hand as if to say, 'Please don't go, I'm only looking round a moment.'

I was hooked! That night at the hotel was busy but I slipped out four or five times to make sure Naughty Face was all right and each time found her standing in her stable busily eating the straw I had so carefully put down as her floor! We didn't get to bed until after 1.00 a.m. and we were woken up by a mournful 'Hee-haw' at six o'clock the next morning. Naughty Face was lonely. As she paced around and around the paddock every now and then giving a mournful bray it became apparent that she needed a companion badly. Mr Morgar had told me of the Donkey Breed Society and I rang up their secretary, Susan Greenway, who advised me to buy another donkey. 'Once you have got two, they will probably settle quite happily and won't be quite so noisy,' she said and recommended a Mrs Joan Spencer who she knew had a donkey for sale. Mrs Spencer came to visit us at the hotel bringing in her loosebox Angelina whom she thought would make a good companion for Naughty Face. She pronounced Naughty Face to be in foal and I was delighted to think that we'd soon have a growing tribe of donkeys, especially when she advised me that Angelina was also in foal.

We became intensely interested in Angelina's and Naughty Face's condition. Naughty Face was a lovely grey colour; Angelina was a deep chocolate brown and Mrs Spencer had told us she had mated her with a white stallion and we could possibly get a broken-coloured donkey, that is one both brown and white. I found myself ringing Susan more and more frequently for advice as we waited in great excitement. Naughty Face had a delightful filly foal named Superdocious but, unfortunately, Angelina's, a deep chocolate-coloured foal, died at birth. I joined the Donkey Breed Society and took up Susan's kind invitation to visit her beautiful stud farm. Niels enjoyed the visit every bit as much as I did and Susan Greenway showed us St Paddy of Kennetbury, a superb stallion, whom we later bought.

Whilst the main reason was our love of donkeys, prices of well-bred stock were reaching as high as £200, and the idea of breeding donkeys was to make a bit of money for ourselves, too.

The flat within the hotel was now far too small for ourselves and the four children. Paul was at boarding school but home for the holidays and Lise was at the local grammar school. We were lucky to purchase the house on ground close to the hotel which had four bedrooms, four acres of land and some stabling facilities. We moved into it in January 1970.

Once we had the land and stabling facilities, I decided to realize an ambition and start breeding seriously. My stud was registered and I became the area representative for the South West for the Donkey Breed Society helping both breeders and donkey-owners with problems. All went well and the donkeys began to build up. Then in December 1970, out of curiosity, I went to visit Exeter Market on a horse sale day. I wandered past the pens of horses, some superb, others looking poor and frightened but all with numbers on and with owners attending them, but right at the fringe of the covered pen where the wagons were unloading I saw a sight which was to change not only my life, but the lives of my husband, four children and many other people whom at that time I was not even aware existed.

It was quite simply a small pen, suitable for two ponies perhaps, into which seven small terrified donkeys were crammed so tightly they could hardly move. Their condition was indescribable, and I was just rooted to the ground in horror. Their coats were long and full of lice, their feet overgrown and twisted and they were all in a state of shock. Several rough-looking men were hanging over the rails and I asked who owned the donkeys. One nodded at a younger man busy talking and I waited impatiently for him to finish.

'How much for that poor donkey there?' I pointed at the worst one. He didn't even look to see which one. 'Forty-five pounds,' he said. I swallowed hard; it looked as if it had only a few days to live and the price was obviously exorbitant. The donkey looked at me and I looked at the donkey. That was it. 'I'll have it,' I said. 'Sorry,' said the young man, 'I've just sold the business to this gentleman here. They're all his now,' and he turned away and disappeared between the wagons.

'Fifty-five pounds,' said the new owner. 'Sorry, take it or leave it.' I walked away from the pen for a few minutes to try and collect my thoughts, before turning back just in time to see the last donkey driven out of the pen and into a lorry, tail twisted cruelly behind him to speed his departure. I had thought too long.

I didn't sleep that night – neither did Niels when I told him what had happened to those donkeys. By chance I did meet the same donkeys again; once again I was unable to help, when an advertisement in the paper for a skewbald donkey mare appeared and we went to see her. She was in a small stable and was not in very good condition although she had beautiful markings. We could hear other donkeys in the next stable but the man told us that all the other donkeys were sold and he wasn't authorized to show us any more. But when he walked off curiosity overcame us and we slipped into the next shed. In the dim light, packed in tightly, were about forty, all in appalling condition. They had no food so Niels broke open four or five bales of hay lying near by which we spread for them and which they started to munch with desperate eagerness. I was sure I recognized my donkey from the market. Neither of us could talk on the way home. We were just shattered and knew something had to be done. Next day, when I rang regarding the broken-coloured donkey, I asked whether I could buy any donkeys from the next stable. There was a short silence, then I was told they were all sold to a donkey sanctuary.

April of the next year finally convinced me of my dedication to donkey welfare. A member of the Donkey Breed Society had asked me if I would help them get a family donkey. They wanted a grey mare about five years old and none of our members had one for sale. Seeing one advertised by a dealer, I arranged for it to be delivered to the Salston so that I could ensure it would prove a sound purchase.

Arriving back from a trip to the cash-and-carry for the hotel, Niels told me the donkey had been delivered and was in the field with the others. Sure enough there she was and I walked over to look her over. She was terrified. I decided not to press my attentions then, thinking it would be better when she joined the others for a feed at tea-time. Still she would not come and we went to bed without having got near her.

The donkeys were noisy in the early morning and dawn had only just broken when we looked through the window to see what

Smartie was lying down in the field

all the fuss was about. The noise was, of course, coming from Naughty Face and Angelina, always 'in charge', and they were standing by an inert grey form in the middle of the field.

'Come on,' I said to Niels, 'that new donkey is in trouble.'

We pulled on old trousers and sweaters and rushed up the field. She lay stretched out, breathing shallowly and unable to get up.

'We'll have to get some help, darling, to carry her down to the shed. She will have to be taken in,' Niels said, but even as he was talking we were both trying to lift her and to our surprise we found we could pick her up between us. She was virtually a living skeleton. Carefully we carried her to a small shed by the back door, laid her on a deep layer of straw and covered her with a blanket. She was no longer frightened, she was too ill.

I heated some milk, thinned it with water, added glucose and gently spooned it down her throat. Niels fixed the infra-red bulb over her, but then he had to go to the hotel for an eight o'clock start. I sat on spooning milk and glucose. The vet arrived and shook his head sadly. 'You've got a real job on,' he said: 'she's almost starved to death.' He gave her a vitamin injection and promised to call the next day. I shook out some fresh tantalizing hay by her head and went inside to ring the dealer who had delivered her. He expressed great surprise; she was 'the best of the lot that arrived'. What could the others have been like, I wondered, asking him to call and see for himself and this he promised to do.

Back in the shed, the donkey had got her head up and to my great joy had a mouthful of hay! I knelt by her and moving the blanket began to brush her gently. Great handfuls of lice-infested hair came away and sore after sore became evident. I was still gently working by lunch-time, but I was winning on one side at least, and the lice powder was surely taking effect. I wished I'd put some on myself! By evening she was standing up, shakily, but up. I gave her a very tiny amount of bran soaked in warm water and black treacle, and this vanished quickly. My younger son, Clive, came in and said, 'She lookes quite different now she's brushed out. Why don't we call her Smartie?' It was a long battle but we won and Smartie joined our herd.

Having the hotel proved a great advantage for the welfare of donkeys. Visitors seeing them in the field made inquiries and were almost always interested, contributing funds, too. Information began to come in as to where donkeys were in distress and an urgent call came one boiling hot August day from a guest at the hotel who was visiting a local resort. 'Mrs Svendsen, I do wish you could come – this poor little donkey has been giving rides all day and has collapsed. They've left it lying at the side of the beach under a sack but it's still alive.'

Niels was away so I jumped in my car and drove off. When I got to the beach the hotel guest was waiting anxiously. 'They've got it in that wagon just leaving,' she said. I followed the wagon and after a few miles it arrived at a rough field. It was met by a man, obviously the owner, who started talking to the driver. He was large and rough. Together they climbed into the back of the lorry. I peered in.

'Excuse me, is that your donkey?' I asked. A stream of bad language emerged to the effect that she was a lazy bag and had ruined his day's trade.

'Can I have a look at her, please?'

'No, clear off, she'll be all right after a rest. Those buggers just need a clout on the head and then they behave. I should have been on the beach myself and not let that young girl have 'em . . . Get up,' he yelled at the donkey and brandished a large stick and struck her on the quarters. I felt sick.

'I'll buy her if you like,' I said. 'She's not much use to you – what do you want for her?'

'She'll be all right when she's had a taste of this,' he said, and struck her again.

'If you strike her again, I'll kill you.'

It stopped him; he laughed. I suppose it was an idle threat but I have never been able to accept violence towards defenceless creatures.

'I'll sell her for forty pounds,' he said.

'I'll give you thirty-five pounds delivered to the Salston Hotel.'

He lifted his stick again. 'All right, forty pounds, but delivered.' My heart was making thumping noises but the donkey had lifted her head and was looking at me. He climbed out of the wagon.

'Where's the cash, then?'

I made out a cheque and scribbled a receipt for him to sign on a piece of paper. The driver set off for Ottery St Mary and as the truck left safely I turned to the owner and said: 'I'll tell the RSPCA of this, and if ever there's a repeat of this ill treatment again I shall be back.'

I passed the wagon and led it home. Niels was there, concerned about my tear-stained face, but as always he understood and helped to gently unload the donkey. Once again the vet hurried out. Once again he shook his head: 'She's about forty-five years old and she's had a heart attack – I'll do my best, but . . .'

In the same little stable in which we had nursed Smartie, the old lady fought for her life, and she *did* fight. We spoon-fed her, she had injections twice a day – and, of course, hot bran mash with black treacle which she was able to enjoy! Three days later she was standing up in the yard. The guest who had rescued her came to have a look. 'She really is a lucky lady now,' she said, and Lucky Lady she became. She improved steadily but was not really able to hold her own with the other donkeys. By this time we had Niels' stepfather, Svend Iversen, living on his own in

42

Exeter and he had a beautiful orchard; he offered to give Lucky Lady a home until she was able to fend for herself. As space was a big problem, this seemed ideal and an extremely close relationship built up between the two. As he obviously never carried a stick, or mistreated her in any way, Lucky Lady began to regain her confidence in human beings, and indeed to get a bit of her own back. He had to be extremely careful only to bring the very best hay into the field – any poor quality material was inspected immediately, and before he had time to get to the gate she would trot in front of him, turn round, and give him a not too gentle kick just to let him know he was not fully appreciated! After three years of this love-hate relationship the orchard was sold and Lucky Lady returned to us. The very sad day came when it was kinder to put her to sleep, a decision we do have to take when the really old donkeys are beginning to suffer.

Locally I became known as the Donkey Lady and found I had gained an overnight reputation of being eccentric, not quite what I was after! By now we seemed to have a sanctuary and information from the Donkey Breed Society and the press indicated there were two similar projects running; one, Miss Philpin's donkey sanctuary near Reading, a registered charity, and the other Mr Lockwood at Godalming who was not registered.

It seemed better to put our activities on a proper footing and after a long time discussing it with the Donkey Breed Society and also with our lawyers, we applied to become a registered charity in October 1972 with Niels and me as trustees and with the approval of the Donkey Breed Society. John Lovell, a great friend and also a lawyer, coped with all the paper work required and in March 1973 the South Western Donkey Sanctuary became registered.

We just didn't have enough room for the number of donkeys that were coming in. Donkeys need quite a large amount of space even for exercise and it was quite obvious that to continue taking in donkeys we were going to need more.

A lot of local interest had been shown in a countryside park which opened within a few miles of the hotel and so I went to see the owner, Mrs Judith Forbes. She was extremely sympathetic and proudly showed me round her lovely park. If I would be

43

prepared to fence and put some buildings up she would be prepared to let me have twelve acres of land for the fitter donkeys to roam on. This seemed like an answer to a prayer and having thanked her I rushed back home to tell Niels.

There he was sitting in his office at the hotel staring miserably at a set of figures he had just got out for the year's turnover. 'I think you had better sit down, darling,' he said. 'And let's both talk about money.'

It was quite obvious to both of us what was happening; any profit which we made from the hotel was quite literally being eaten by the donkeys. There just weren't enough funds to do the necessary fencing at Farway and unless I was able to start organizing finances on my own for the donkeys we wouldn't be able to take any more in *and* keep the hotel going. We desperately needed three more stables at Salston Close to look after the fit donkeys we had and the first quotation for the fencing was £600. We spent a very worrying week trying to work out ways of raising more funds and then suddenly help appeared.

Rosalind de Wesselow, a fellow member of the Donkey Breed Society, had a good friend, Colonel Gerald Critchley of the Home of Rest for Horses. They also had a great interest in donkeys and thanks to Rosalind's help, and a trip on my part to London, the home very kindly agreed to pay our fencing costs! That gave us the encouragement we so badly needed to keep going.

At this time the *Down Your Way* team from the long-established radio programme visiting different towns in different parts of the country arrived in Ottery, and I was rather amused on their arrival. They signed in at the reception desk of our hotel where they were staying to do the programme and asked me behind the desk, assuming I was the receptionist, 'We hear there is an eccentric donkey lady lives somewhere near here. Could you tell us where we could contact her?'

After a few embarrassing moments it was all cleared up and they did an interview which focused the attention of donkey lovers throughout the country on the work we were struggling to do on our own.

A disturbing result of the programme was that five more donkeys arrived, their owners having taken note of our address.

One was a walking skeleton; she became Twiggy, naturally! She arrived as we were building our new 'isolation block' of stables. We were learning fast, each new arrival seemed to spread a different ailment around our population and it seemed new families of lice were ready and willing to change owners at a minute's notice. We developed a system so that each arrival was put in the isolation block for a period of three weeks.

During this period of time the most important thing was to get the confidence of the donkey. Donkeys like Twiggy, who had been starved almost to the point of death, had also frequently been mistreated and before we could start making any real physical improvement we had to help them to regain their faith in human beings. It always seemed worth while when I had time to stand quietly in a box gently stroking the muzzle of a donkey which had probably never known any kindness before in its life. And Twiggy survived.

So many of them were covered with bleeding sores and infested with lice and I found it very hard to accept that human beings had inflicted such terrible hardship on poor innocent creatures. I loved them.

When a new donkey arrived, the vet called as soon as he could to give the donkeys a full medical check and we also had a visit from the farrier as mostly the donkey's feet were absolutely appalling and until they were pared back so the donkeys could stand properly they suffered considerable discomfort and pain. Some arrivals could barely walk and my heart would sink as I saw them lurching from the lorries. I kept a tightly fitting head-scarf and a polo-necked shirt at the ready and started to groom the donkeys to clear the lice. With the children, of course, I had got used to tidemarks round the bath but I had to try to get used to lice marks after my work was done. The lice never seemed to bite or to irritate me but it's hard to get used to the feeling of being crawled over.

The very large lumps of matted hair had to be cut out patiently and a large pair of kitchen scissors came in handy. Many a shaggy coat was tangled beyond hope and with running sores beneath the only way to prevent further suffering was to clip the coat bit by bit with scissors until the tangle was free. I always talk quietly whilst I work and the donkeys never seem to mind or grow impatient. Somehow they seem to appreciate what is being done. Now, with some donkeys, we have progressed to electric clippers which are much quicker and more efficient; but I still wonder which the donkeys really prefer.

I was still breeding a few donkeys using St Paddy as the stud stallion and of course only using mares which we had bought for the purpose. We sold our foals when they got to eight or nine months old and the money raised by getting them to good homes for a good price helped to keep the sanctuary running. Angelina and Naughty Face each had another beautiful foal. Niels and I saw an advertisement in the paper one day for a 'pink or strawberry roan donkey' for sale. Even Niels was quite excited at the thought of this unusual colour and so off we went to Sticklepath to buy Bambi who was to become my husband's favourite donkey. She was indeed the most beautiful strawberry roan colour and on her arrival back at home we lost little time in putting her to the stallion. Supremo was born one year later and was the first pink and white donkey born in the country. He received a tremendous reception!

Occasionally, going round to shows, I met members of the Donkey Breed Society, all of whom were interested in the work I was doing on the welfare side. Priscilla Kirby, who is a very well known breeder and member of the Society, rang me one night at home to say that she had a terrible problem. She had sold two of her favourite donkeys called Rosanna and Black Coffee to what she had taken to be an extremely good home – a wealthy director of some large city finance outfit, who had plenty of land. Rosanna had been a show donkey until Priscilla had sold her, and Black Coffee, her daughter, was a large donkey with the gentlest nature imaginable. Like many good stud owners, Priscilla went to visit her donkeys in their new homes just after a year. To her horror both Rosanna and Black Coffee were desperately lame, thin and frightened and they had had no farrier all the time they had been there. She threatened the owner with prosecution unless he let her have them. Could I possibly take them because they were in such terrible condition she didn't feel she could cope with them in her stud and she would pay their expenses to get them down to me, she asked.

Within a very short time Rosanna and Black Coffee arrived. It took us three years to get them right. It was amazing how thin and emaciated they had become in one year of neglect and it made me worried that I occasionally *had* to sell my foals to make sufficient money to keep the sanctuary running.

In January 1973, Bob Forbes, a well-known interviewer on BBC *Spotlight* rang to say he would like to come down and do an interview with me and the donkeys. They would arrive in one and a half hours! Feeling a bit shattered, we bustled around and, true enough, a minibus arrived laden to the roof with men and cameras.

'Right, we want a good *hee-haw* noise to start with,' said Bob Forbes, and the sound man, the camera man and all the other men stood in silence outside the stable block waiting hopefully. Of course, donkeys *can* be stubborn occasionally, and one hour later we were all still waiting.

'Right,' said Bob, 'get all the donkeys together and I'll do an interview.'

I explained that some donkeys were rescued mares and never

Paddy took a great interest in the TV man's coat

mixed with our pedigree stock who were fit to have foals, or with St Paddy. He was in the most presentable, easily accessible paddock with his three wives and three children and so we featured him.

The man responsible for sound, Tony Turner, was wearing one of those very long hairy Afghan coats, a sort of motley brown colour, and he set himself up carefully with his gear, behind Bob Forbes and facing me. Time was spent arranging 'the set' – a large rack of hay was by me, and all the mares and foals gathered around to enjoy the action.

A little clapperboard man sprang in front of me and the show was on. It felt most unreal, as Bob Forbes said in his BBC voice, 'Mrs Svendsen, what made you *start* looking after donkeys?'

I tried to concentrate and answer clearly, but behind Bob and the camera I could see St Paddy – he was pawing the ground and snorting. I could hear the camera running and a microphone and boom was dangling on a long pole one foot above my head.

'But why donkeys?' insisted Bob Forbes. I was just explaining what gentle creatures they were when my eyes became riveted on to St Paddy. My voice faded as he started his charge – he had decided the sound man was a new mare and obviously he had a duty to perform. There was a muffled shriek behind Bob, and the sound man collapsed!

The film was finished by late afternoon and I sank into a chair exhausted. But within half an hour the telephone had rung again, 'This is Westward TV. Angela Rippon would like to come and do a film of you and your donkeys.'

'Oh no!' I replied. 'The BBC have been here all day – you're too late.'

'We shall film in colour,' they said. 'How about nine in the morning?' But their film men wore more conventional coats, so there were no problems.

The two films came out very well, the donkeys were marvellous and the hee-haw which heralded both performances was achieved in the end. To get a good sound effect I just did my early morning call of 'Donkeys!' ' as I came to the stables, rattling the feed buckets – it never failed.

By this time the hotel's gardener, Herb Fry, had given up any pretence of doing the hotel's garden – with the stud donkeys, and the rescued donkeys, we had reached the amazing figure of thirty-eight and they took some looking after. Fit donkeys need great care to remain in peak condition but sickly, malnourished donkeys need constant daily individual attention. Cleaning out, feeding, grooming, veterinary work, plus trying to help Niels build up the hotel, was becoming almost impossible. People wanting to help started to send donations and every donor needed a personal reply as the money was so desperately needed and I really was so grateful. A large donation from friends nearby really made an impact on our finances.

Herb and I worked marvellously together – a true Devonshire man, he had a good knowledge of farming and animals and his gentleness and feeling for the sick animals was apparent. He was much stronger physically than I was and in 1971 he became a full-time donkey person.

At one meeting of the DBS council the name of Violet Philpin came up. She ran the donkey sanctuary whose full name was in fact the Helping Hand Animal Welfare League Donkey Sanctuary, near Reading, and was the subject of a fair amount of concern amongst council members. She was very elderly and was looking after 200 to 250 donkeys which she had bought in from dealers all over the country. Niels and I decided to visit her. A more dedicated and devoted person we could never meet, she loved every one of her donkeys. But what of their fate if anything happened to her? She must have been eighty-one on our first visit and she was in deep financial difficulties. She had trouble with the dealers from whom she bought her donkeys, and we promised to help in any way we could.

Only an hour after we got home that evening she phoned to ask if we could take six 'very bad' donkeys that had just been delivered from Reading market. She felt she just couldn't cope because they were in such a state, and she would send the wagon straight on to us, plus fifty pounds to help cover our costs. By 3 a.m. it arrived. On board were the donkeys we named Biddy, Black Beauty, Bill and Ben, So Shy and Tiny Titch. Their condition was indescribable – Niels and my eldest children, Lise and Paul, helped them into the biggest stable which I had emptied in readiness and we all stood quietly in the early morning light in shocked silence. None of the donkeys could move alone and their spirits seemed completely broken.

The driver was sitting where we left him in the kitchen, with a cup of coffee. I said, 'Poor little donkeys – they're in terrible condition.'

'Naw,' he replied. 'Reading market isn't as bad as Southall – you should see 'em there! They'll be all right in a week or so – you'll see.' I suddenly wanted to be rid of him. 'It's disgusting,' I said quietly. 'You should be ashamed to even transport them.' He stood up in a menacing fashion. 'Here. I'm just the driver and they're just bloody donkeys. Get off *my* back,' and he left the kitchen without drinking his coffee.

Niels and the children were still talking quietly to the donkeys and fed each a little bran mash. We only dared let them have a morsel as too much can cause severe colic and in any event it was all they could manage. The slight interest shown on being given a warm meal was enough reward for all of us for the night so we turned out the light and a very subdued and sad family got to sleep around 4 a.m.

There was the usual early-morning dash to get breakfast and get the children off to school and it was eight o'clock before I was ready to go out to see the early morning delivery. Herb was waiting for me at the back door. His kindly face wrinkled up with concern. From being a young boy he had always worked on farms and been with animals. To him farm animals had a simple purpose in life. They were bred carefully, reared properly and when their time came culled for human consumption. This was the way of the farmer, and Herb fully approved.

In the light of the morning we stood looking at the donkeys. 'Tin't right,' he said. 'Look at that poor little beggar's back.' The smallest donkey was shivering in the corner – his back was bent from cowering at the frequent beatings that had been his lot and the hair looked solid and peculiar. The solid lumps on Tiny Titch were pieces of sacking embedded in his back with small broken pieces of spine showing through. He was only about eight months old. I cried and so did Herb. Could Tiny Titch stand the anaesthetic the vet would need to give him to remove the sacking, and could we mend his splintered spine? With the vet, we decided to let him recover a little first, and put him in one of the smaller stables with the poor little thin terrified mare, So Shy.

With the vet and Herb's help I was able to touch So Shy gently and look at her teeth to find her age. *All* her front teeth were broken, congealed blood still on the gums. She had been beaten as badly as Tiny Titch. The vet gave her an anaesthetic straight away, as she could not possibly eat with her mouth in that condition, and we removed five chipped and broken teeth and sewed up her lacerated gums. The only good thing was that they were her milk teeth, and, with luck, new ones should replace them. We covered her with a rug and fondled her as she came round. Poor So Shy, what a start!

The two stallions were both huddled together and we named them Bill and Ben; they would have to be gelded when strong enough. The other two mares consisted of a tiny middle-aged brown one we named Biddy, and a jet-black mare we named Black Beauty.

There is a happy ending to this story – So Shy and Tiny Titch recovered fully with us – and fell quietly in love! When they were better I found them a wonderful home in Devon and arranged with the new owners that Tiny Titch be gelded when he was really strong, the sanctuary paying. They did this when he was two, but just a little too late! So Shy produced a beautiful little foal one year after and she is embarrassingly friendly now!

As we were now a registered charity, proper books had to be kept and each evening would find me making careful records of the donations received and the expenses involved. We put a collecting box on the reception desk at the hotel and guests were extremely kind; it was amazing how much money this would collect over a week's period. I wrote our first leaflet. Having commandeered one of the old typewriters from the hotel and had it roneoed off, all the children helped in the evening by putting letters in envelopes and putting stamps on. Everyone who had sent a donation received a leaflet.

The donations trickled in. With the average cost per donkey at £2.50 a week, and the ever-increasing numbers of donkeys, our capital had nearly filtered away. We had wanted a skiing holiday with the children but just didn't have the funds available.

Quite a large number of visitors came to the sanctuary and many offered to take the donkeys and keep them in their own homes. It would be a good idea, we thought, provided the homes selected were ideal. The first essential was that the donkeys were genuinely wanted for their own sake and not as riding donkeys on the cheap for their children. We worked out a legal arrangement whereby a selected home which was willing to take preferably two donkeys, gave a donation of between five and twenty pounds to us and agreed to keep the donkeys in good condition on a permanent basis. I would always visit the home before the donkeys went out and thereafter every six months to ensure that they were looking after the donkeys properly. If for any reason the owners could not keep the donkeys they were to be returned as they were the sanctuary's property at all times and they could never be sold by their temporary owners.

This scheme helped tremendously to keep our numbers down to a reasonable level and with the fitter ones being transferred to Farway and the sick ones remaining with us we managed.

That April we were phoned by the RSPCA. A very elderly blind man in a small village on the edge of Dartmoor had to go into hospital and his donkey would be left alone – would we take it in?

Niels and I set off in our Land-Rover and trailer and found ourselves eventually in a dirty farmyard, seemingly totally deserted. We blew the horn, checked it was the right address, and then sat rigid as a donkey slowly waddled towards us! It was *enormous*. It was so fat, particularly after our usual starved customers, we just could not believe our eyes! 'Jenny,' came a voice from the house, 'Jenny, come here.' She waddled slowly past us up to the back door of the house. An old blind man was struggling to tip a sack of cow cake into the tub by the door. 'Let me help,' said Niels. 'Ho, are you here for Jenny?' he said, and a tear trickled slowly down his old sightless face.

'Yes,' said Niels. 'We'll take the greatest care of her.'

'I've no one, you see – it's the end for me – I've lived here nearly eighty years – old Jenny's kept me company since my wife died thirty years ago.' He turned and went into the house.

Niels and I looked at each other. 'Let's load her up quick,' Niels said. 'It's only going to hurt him if we hang about.'

What a job – talk about two-ton Tessy, she only just fitted into the trailer and she didn't want to go in!

'You'll feed her properly now, won't you,' said the old man. He was standing by the door. 'For the last ten years since I lost my sight, I've just kept her bin full of cow cake and she's helped herself.'

I held his hand and said, 'Don't worry, I promise we will look after her all her life.'

I couldn't bear to see him standing there, the tears running uncontrollably down his face and ran back to the Land-Rover. Niels, Jenny and I went slowly home. We called her Fat Jenny as we already had a Jenny, and a slimmer and more energetic version of herself is still happily with us.

Then came Amanda, the result of another desperate call from Miss Philpin, which produced a late-night lorry of donkeys. This one was a miniature donkey, with a very kind nature. She was so gentle she would nuzzle and cuddle up every time we went in the stable. We put her on a maximum feed as soon as we were able, as it was obvious she was heavily in foal. She had a terrible time when the foal was due, but eventually the vet and I knelt on the straw desperately trying to get the little colt to breathe. We succeeded, but he was so tiny and his back legs did not seem just right. We named him Peanuts.

Amanda was a wonderful mother and for four weeks she cared and loved him, and then disaster – I did my normal round just before going to bed and on opening Amanda's door found her lying dead. I desperately listened for sounds through my stethoscope and massaged her heart, but to no avail – Peanuts was an orphan at four weeks old.

We carried him into the kitchen and he slept by our Aga that night. We had to mix a milk solution with the right amount of water, calcium hydroxide and glucose to suit him. His legs were poor due to bone malformation, but he was such a happy little chap. We made plaster casts for his little legs and changed them every week. But then he began to slip backwards on us – his weight dropped and he became apathetic. At this time we had another foal in trouble – a mare suddenly rejected her colt named Pancho. For his own safety we moved him away from her and in with Peanuts. Then a marvellous thing happened. Angelina with St Dougal (one of St Paddy's legitimate offspring) was grazing next to the nursery box and showed great interest in the foals. With my heart in my mouth I let her into the box with Peanuts and Pancho and she went straight up to them and nuzzled them both and within seconds *both* were suckling! That was the turning point for Peanuts – plaster casts no longer worried him and every morning he would leave Angelina and come with me to the kitchen, lie quietly on the table whilst his casts were taken off and his leg was dressed and then go happily back to Angelina, who brought up the three foals until they were all eight months old!

Poor Amanda! Part of the post-mortem report read: 'The fatty degeneration of the liver was, in my opinion, probably due to the fact that this donkey had been previously undernourished and had maintained herself and her foal, which she produced alive a month previously, at the expense of her body fat reserves.'

One of our big problems has always been the long gestation period of the donkey, from eleven to thirteen months. This means that despite having changed a starving mare into a reasonably fit animal, the damage has been done to the vital organs, and the production of a foal during the difficult early months means we cannot always win.

What with the family and our large tribe of donkeys there was little time for housework, which has never been my biggest love, and I always managed to get somebody to help me with that. Cooking I really do enjoy. We are a great games family and every night would find us playing Monopoly, Totopoly or Mah-jong. My parents had moved to Ottery St Mary from the North in 1973 and enjoyed evenings with us. Our favourite annual holiday was to go back to the Norfolk Broads and each year my parents would take one motor boat and Niels and I with our children would take either one or two yachts and we would spend a delightful carefree week sailing the northern rivers which we loved. Herb was able to look after the sanctuary during my absence and the vets used to visit daily so that we could get away.

I absolutely loved the sailing and Niels and I agreed that we would take a navigation course together in our spare time and that I would take my radio operator's licence which I felt might be of some use in the future. Taking a navigation course from home was quite fun and a terrific change from my normal day's work. We both got through our course and did an examination taken on the boat to get our radio operators' licences.

It was extremely convenient living within a hundred yards of one's business and every Sunday evening found me at the Salston both winter and summer. Early on with Keith and Mo, Sunday had been the slackest night of the week. We decided on a candle-lit night and some music to interest people and advertised the Salston's Candlelit Bar. The four of us sat waiting for the anticipated crowds. By half past nine there wasn't one person there and we were all getting desperate. At that moment a car drew in and four people appeared in the doorway.

'What's on, then?' said a voice from the North. 'A power cut?' and he leered round the bar which was dimly lit by candles.

'No,' said Niels and explained.

The man gazed into the gloom, looking at the empty chairs and tables. 'Tisn't working, is it,' he said. 'I'll have a pint of beer,' and he slurped over with his pint and sat down with his family at one of the empty tables.

I don't know why but it seemed to put us all on our mettle and we decided that we would concentrate on trying to get Sunday nights going. We had seen advertised a group calling themselves the Accordionnaires and we asked them to come over for an interview. Cliff and Margaret duly arrived the following Sunday and gave an extremely lively performance using their accordions. Just for a joke I borrowed their microphone and sang a little song. 'Wonderful,' they said; 'why don't we try this on a Sunday and see if this gets the crowds in.' And so Salston Singalong Night started. We even got Niels singing 'I was born under a wandering star', which became a firm favourite with all the regulars and that Christmas was quite fantastic with over two hundred and fifty people attending, the Ottery St Mary Handbell Ringers and school choirs coming to make it an evening to remember. Although it was always very tiring it was a great change and Niels and I always enjoyed ourselves.

Just after we returned from the Norfolk Broads in May 1973, Maud arrived. Of all the comedians ever to walk into the sanctuary, Maud was the best. She almost equalled Houdini for escapology, despite her thirty-five years, but never went anywhere! *Hee-haw*, *hee-haw*, right under our window, between two and four any morning, meant she had done it again – and there she would stand, waiting patiently for us to come down and put her back into her stable so that she could repeat the episode!

She had arrived with a bad attack of pneumonia, and to keep her exercised I used to put a halter on her and we would amble up the drive to the hotel and round the track which was known as Salston Ride. She would enjoy eating the tasty thistles that thrived there. It became a habit when she was better for our neighbour's children to take Maud for a walk, and this she adored.

Dr Jeremy Bradshaw-Smith lived at the far end of Salston Ride and his daughter Lucy and our Sarah frequently took Maud on her walks. One hot summer day the phone rang – it was the doctor. 'Your donkey is in my garden,' he started. I looked in the lounge and there were Sarah and Lucy playing but they must have forgotten Maud. Oh dear – desperately I searched for excuses – apologies. 'Can she stay, please?' the doctor was saying. 'She's doing a marvellous job, she's going steadily round the edge of the lawn eating off the pieces the mower won't get to.' After that Maud was frequently in demand as the local lawnmower.

On one occasion she was 'mowing' the hotel's putting green, working efficiently round the edges. Two rather elderly ladies were playing a serious game of putting, and Niels, talking to the head waiter in the dining room, noticed her ambling across to see what was going on. Intent on their game, her arrival went unnoticed until she decided one of the players needed a little assistance, and what obviously seemed a gentle friendly nudge to Maud was enough, administered in the right place at the right time, to put the guest completely off her stroke. Fortunately they took it in good part and Maud was allowed to join in officially after that! She never really disgraced herself, however, and would always wander quietly back home when her job for the day was done.

But we needed money and so put an advertisement in the *Sunday Telegraph* which read:

Help a little donkey in distress . . . Recently started Donkey Sanctuary in desperate need of funds to help with the rescue and rehabilitation of not only the old and sick, but unfortunately also the young and ill-treated donkey. Donations, please, to the South Western Donkey Sanctuary, Ottery St Mary, Devon.

The response to this was quite amazing, and I had a terrible job trying to reply to the many inquiries and letters, particularly as at that time Gyppo arrived. Miss Philpin telephoned from Reading and, even for her, she was unusually quiet. 'I've got such a dreadful case in, I don't really think I can cope . . . can you take in an old donkey covered with sores, and with her feet cut to ribbons? She has been working on a used car dump in Middlesex and has had a chain harness on, and been driven up piles of wrecked cars, and then had to pull bits the gypsies wanted all the way down again . . . the RSPCA rescued her and have sent her to me. I just feel I can't cope and rather than unload her from this wagon, I'll send her straight on. *Please* will you take her, you are my only hope?' Herb and I prepared a stable.

You think you are ready for anything but when that wagon came and the back was opened, and we saw that donkey lying there, her feet bleeding, running sores on her chest and quarters where the chains had cut, and her desperate frightened eyes, I was close to tears. We had to carry her, she could not walk, and we laid her on the deep bed of straw and covered her with a woollen rug so that she could rest after the journey.

The wagon driver passed me an envelope and I was overjoyed to find a hundred pounds in one-pound notes in it sent by Miss Philpin to help us. Although she was in dire financial straits herself she recognized our terrible financial problems and was so grateful to us for taking her worst cases as she must have realized her strength was failing and she couldn't carry on much longer.

We named her Gyppo, in doubtful honour of her past owners, and despite her previous treatment she had the gentlest, kindest nature. She lay down for three weeks . . . we turned her regularly to prevent her getting bed-sores and her feet were bathed and bandaged twice a day. Her chest and rump wounds were bad and we found an ointment called Dermobian that worked wonders. And she had injections of antibiotics to prevent further infection.

Our joy when she felt able to stand made up for the long days we had spent with her . . . she tottered round her stable and could reach the hay for herself. I got four large plastic ice cream containers and twice a day half-filled them with a saline solution in warm water and Savlon. Once she got the idea that one was for each foot, she showed the most amazing intelligence; gently she would step into each, and stand for hours, a blissful expression on her face, gently chewing hay from the net we hung within reach! Visitors found it hilariously funny, but we never laughed at her, though we sometimes had to laugh with her, as she began to find life worth living again. The first day we were able to let her go into the grassy paddock was memorable. Her obvious delight, and the fact that after a brief look round, a sample of the grass and a brief rub against a nearby tree, she returned to the gate and gave me a quick nuzzle before doing her lovely victory roll in the sandpatch we always provided, showed her gratitude and her way of giving thanks. She lived for a glorious four years before dying a natural, peaceful death with us around her.

I now began to make regular visits up to Farway to supervise the fencing of the area loaned to us by Mrs Forbes. We needed shelters as well before we could put the donkeys there as it was very open exposed land and apart from individual stables, an area where we could store food and hay necessary for feeding the donkeys. I got a local firm of contractors from Ottery St Mary who had built the stables at Salston Close to erect the stables at Farway and I was extremely grateful when they were all completed and we were able to take our first donkeys up to graze in the Farway Countryside Park. It was wonderful having Mrs Forbes and Morris look after them for us and every evening I would slip up with the children to make sure that everything was going well.

We managed to pay for the shelters from the money coming in regularly now from the *Telegraph* advertisements. One or two really large donations came in at this period which were very welcome but we were beginning to realize that we needed much more room if we were to continue.

We saw in the paper that a farm was for sale at Teignmouth and Niels and I drove out to see if it was any use to us. It would have been ideal, the long sheds which had been used for caged minks were just high enough to house donkeys and we reckoned that we could winter almost one hundred donkeys there if we had to. However, something had to be done rather desperately and we asked how much the owner wanted for his farm. We were absolutely horrified to find it was almost £1,000 an acre. There was no way we could arrange this sort of finance and we were both very depressed to be told that this was the sort of price we would have to pay to buy agricultural land in our district. On approaching various land agents we found this was only too true.

Miss Philpin had made a habit of ringing me late in the evening to ask if I could take donkeys that had got into trouble. Poor Miss Philpin, she was obviously deeply concerned over her inability due to failing health to take in more animals in need, and it can't have helped her when I poured out my troubles and problems and inability to find sufficient finance I needed to buy a large enough property to cope with the incoming number of donkeys. She was very sympathetic one night on the phone and said, 'Never mind, dear, I'm sure it will turn out all right and you never know I may be able to help,' at the same time asking me to take six small donkeys.

The donkey rehabilitation scheme was working, although not without its difficulties. Not all prospective owners agreed with my conditions to take the donkeys. Most had no qualms in filling in the questionnaire I had designed and giving a donation but one irate lady took it very badly. 'How dare you ask for money when I am prepared to give one of your donkeys a good home? You should be extremely grateful that I am willing to help. And why should I take two? I have only one daughter so who is going to ride the other one, tell me that?'

Another difficult interview was with a husband and wife who

turned up and offered to take a couple of donkeys. But they had to be a matching pair of greys, between nine and ten hands, be biddable at all times, and strong enough to give daily rides to their two sons, aged eight and ten.

I escaped inside mumbling about finding forms and when I had gained control of my temper found them in the stables with Naughty Face, Angelina and St Paddy.

'We'll have these two, even though the colours are wrong,' they said. 'Can you arrange for a cattle lorry to bring them down?'

No way were they going to take Naughty Face and Angelina, but I gave them the forms and questionnaire. 'My God,' said the husband, 'it is easier to adopt a baby than a donkey.' Whereupon he tore the form into tiny pieces and they left in grim silence. And to add insult to injury they backed their large Jaguar car over our front lawn.

Many good offers of homes did come in and it was difficult at times to go and inspect them. My sister Pat, who lived in Bristol, offered to help when a good home was offered in her area. An elderly lady rang one night to say that she and her two spinster sisters were prepared to give a home to three donkeys, and assured me that they would be well looked after for the rest of their lives. Pat took the address and rang me the next evening. She was ecstatic! 'Bet,' she said, 'it's unbelievable, it's an enormous house, it stands in beautiful grounds with fenced paddocks, walled gardens, and a complete stable block built for ten racehorses and the original grooms who keep them spotless, despite the fact that there have been no horses there since their father died fifteen years ago! From the stable boy up, and he's in his mid-seventies, they would all love the donkeys, and there's nothing they wouldn't have. We couldn't get a better home for them!'

Bill and Ben, who had now been gelded, had made friends with another gelding named Boots, and these we selected for the three elderly ladies. They were duly delivered, and received with all the love and attention they could wish for. I telephoned in mid-summer to find all was absolutely marvellous, each sister had her own favourite, and the donkeys were good as gold. It was a great relief to know they were settled and I was surprised to receive a desperate telephone call in December.

'Mrs Svendsen, I am sorry but you will *have* to take Bill and Ben back; they've got to be such naughty boys. Boots can stay, he's such a good little boy,' the voice continued, 'but we just cannot cope any longer with the other two.'

'I am so sorry,' I said. 'Whatever are they up to?'

'They have got so disobedient, Boots goes straight up the stairs when we tell him, but no matter how we push and pull, Bill and Ben refuse to go up. You know we are elderly ladies, Mrs Svendsen, we can't be expected to do such heavy work.'

I paused. 'Did you say *up* the stairs?' I asked.

'But of course . . . you don't think that we can lie upstairs in our warm beds at night and leave those three little pets in their stables, do you?' The slightly irate voice answered, 'It gets cold, you know – they use the guest bedroom.'

And so regretfully back came Bill and Ben, followed one month later by Boots, who ceased to be angelic when his little friends departed!

The twentieth of June was Niels' birthday, this was 1974, and we came back from an enjoyable celebration at eleven fifteen in the evening. Clive's head popped round the bedroom door, 'That you, Mum? There's a very important message. Whatever time you get in tonight you've got to ring this number and it's very urgent.'

He gave me a Reading telephone number and still in a slightly merry state I wandered down to my little office, Niels behind me. I rang the number and a voice answered, 'Mrs Svendsen? Mrs Elisabeth Doreen Svendsen?'

'Yes,' I replied.

'This is Mr Holman from the Barclay Trust – are you sitting down, Mrs Svendsen?'

I sat down, feeling suddenly very sober. 'Mrs Svendsen, you have been left a legacy.' Visions of thousands of pounds floated across my mind – I'd never had a legacy before.

'How wonderful,' I said. 'How much?'

'Mrs Svendsen,' said the voice. 'It's two hundred and four donkeys!'

4 The legacy

I must have gone very pale because suddenly Niels' arm was round my shoulder. Mr Holman hadn't stopped talking. 'I am sorry to advise you that Miss Philpin of Reading has died,' he continued, 'and you have been named as a residuary legatee. She has made a special clause relating to the donkeys and this is that you are to take as many as you can and those you're unable to take are to be shot.'

I broke in, 'Oh, you can't do that, whatever you do. You mustn't shoot any donkeys.' But Mr Holman's voice was still continuing. 'We should like to know what arrangements you would like to make for Miss Philpin's funeral and whether you would like her to be buried or cremated.'

I was aware of Niels saying, 'What, darling, what's happened? What's going on?' and I silently passed the telephone to him and sat with my head in my hands.

Obviously Niels was getting the same information as I had

Bill and Ben refused to go upstairs

received and I have never seen him looking so worried in his life. Niels tapped me, 'Darling, he wants to know what we are to feed them on tomorrow,' weakly, and passed the telephone back to me.

'Mr Holman,' I said. 'Is there no food there at all?'

Mr Holman cleared his throat and said, 'Um, about twenty-five bales of hay, Mrs Svendsen, and then there is nothing.'

I sat thinking for a moment. 'Mr Holman, there's no way you can shoot the donkeys,' I said again.

After promising to phone the following morning I rang off and Niels and I sat looking at each other. It had to be a nightmare, I was convinced it couldn't really be happening, but Niels, with his practical side never deserting him, suddenly said, 'I think it's time for a cup of coffee,' and we went into the kitchen and made the strongest cup of coffee with the most sugar in I think I have ever had.

Two hundred and four donkeys seemed an absolutely impossible number but we knew we had to find a way to take them in. Most of the night was spent discussing the problems and regretting the questions that we hadn't asked at the time. It seemed that every card in the pack was stacked against us and I don't think either of us slept very much.

Every morning at half past seven the children (all of them) came into our bed. Fortunately we invested in a big square bed early on in our marriage and we all enjoyed the early morning romp before school started. This morning, however, was different and the children immediately sensed that something was wrong when they came into the bedroom. 'Whatever are you going to do, Mummy?' said Lise, sitting on the bed, her face glum with concern. 'My goodness,' said Paul. 'Where can we put two hundred and four donkeys?' 'I'll have one in my room,' said Sarah happily, who thought it was all a great joke.

But none of them could raise a smile from Niels or me. The first thing Niels said was, 'You'll have to let me do all the hotel work and you will have to concentrate on the donkeys. I'll help as much as I can but obviously one of us will have to keep the business going, otherwise there'll be no money for anybody. Just keep telephoning me and let me know what's happening today and I will be home for lunch as soon as I can,' and so saying Niels got up quietly and went up to the hotel.

'Would you like Miss Philpin buried or cremated?' was Mr Holman's first question when I rang later on. 'Has she no relatives at all?' I queried. 'Surely somebody must know her better than me. I have only met her twice.'

'I am sorry. No,' said Mr Holman. 'You're the only residuary legatee with one or two very small exceptions; everything's been left to you.'

'Oh dear,' I replied. 'In that case I think probably we'd better bury her and then if at a later stage we find she would have wished to be cremated or any relatives appear that can give us guidance, we can always have another service.'

'Very well,' said Mr Holman. 'I will arrange for a church service at Woodley Church where she lived.'

'Could you tell me a little more about the financial situation?' I asked somewhat anxiously. There was Miss Philpin's house, Springfield, which was in fact a very derelict cottage. Her own private account was overdrawn, as was the Helping Hand Animal Welfare League Donkey Sanctuary and some £8,400 was owing. A demand had been made to the executors by a Mr Light for payment for donkeys and some of Miss Philpin's employees had already phoned to ask about back pay due and wages for recent work. The Barclays Bank Trust had been made executors of the will and they would for the time being collect any assets of the charity which might appear and pay any pressing bills out of money that was received.

I walked slowly up to the hotel and sat in Niels' office telling him what had happened. 'Well,' he said, 'you must go to Reading as soon as possible and try and sort things out. It's going to be impossible from here until you've actually seen the situation for yourself.'

And so, very miserably, I went home and packed a suitcase, said goodbye to the children and drove to Reading. I booked in at a local hotel and first thing in the morning went round to meet Mr Holman and his assistant, Miss Jarrett. They were both exceptionally nice and I felt much happier once we could all sit together talking the problem over. Mr Holman, bless him, had made all the arrangements for the funeral and I arranged for two wreaths to be sent, one a very simple wreath of palm leaves with the inscription, 'From all her donkeys', and the other 'From Mr and Mrs Svendsen to the donkeys' true friend'.

The next morning was the funeral and I did wish Niels had been able to come but somebody had to look after the children, the hotel and the donkeys. The funeral was extremely sad and very pathetic; I knew nobody there and as chief mourner it was a very peculiar situation. The vicar gave public words of praise for a woman who had devoted almost the whole of her eighty-three years of life to the donkeys and who had worked through a personal fortune and had died in total poverty.

Mr Holman and I drove out to the sanctuary together and I was quite horrified to see that there weren't in fact 204 donkeys, rather more like eighty or ninety. What had happened to the rest? Most of them were being boarded out, it seemed, in various parts of the country such as Wales and Bristol, and the people who were looking after them were being paid between two and three pounds per donkey per week for their care. This meant bills coming in to the sanctuary weekly and there were, of course, no funds available at all to meet them. Mr Rivers, who had been in charge of the donkeys, was willing to stay on for some weeks and I agreed to pay his wages myself. We arranged for the vet to keep an eye on the donkeys until I was able to get them back to Ottery St Mary. There was in fact enough hay for two or three weeks, no hard feed at all and nowhere near sufficient grass since the whole sanctuary was being run over only about sixteen acres of land.

To add to the confusion it appeared that Miss Philpin was already being sued for the grazing rights because she hadn't paid the rent for some months. After lunch we drove out to Spring-field, Miss Philpin's home. There is no way I can describe the derelict cottage. At one time some ten years ago Miss Philpin had also looked after stray dogs and there was ample evidence that they had inhabited the house. A camp bed lay in one room with a candle on a saucer next to it and the only furniture was up-turned tea chests. A candle and small primus cooking stove stood on another tea chest and in this one room Miss Philpin must have lived. The stench was indescribable.

By the time all the debts were paid off and the house sold there wasn't going to be much left in the kitty, but hopefully enough to meet the new demands now coming in.

It was absolutely amazing over the next few days how many telephone calls and letters came from people claiming Miss Philpin had owed them money. It seemed endless and it was so difficult to determine the genuine claims from those obviously trying it on. A telephone call from the Charity Commissioners in London advised me on the best way to settle these problems and they were immensely helpful, arranging for one of their assistant commissioners to come down to go through my books and to talk to me.

He arrived on 26 June and it was very clear that the Charity Commission were concerned to ensure that the affairs of the Helping Hand Animal Welfare League Donkey Sanctuary were put into working order. He told me that letters had been written to Miss Philpin pleading with her to appoint new trustees to assist in her difficulties but by then Miss Philpin had reached the stage and age when small matters like this to her just didn't count as long as she could keep her donkeys going; she had died before appointing new trustees.

The obvious desperate need was to bring the eighty-four donkeys from Reading to Devon and so our charity wrote formally offering the help of the South Western Donkey Sanctuary under special terms agreeable to Barclays Trust as executors and to the Charity Commissioners. We would amalgamate the two charities and Niels and I would have another two trustees so that we had a sound basis on which to work. Judith Forbes and Rosalind de Wesselow who were already helping us both agreed and we were delighted.

After the commissioner left I went for a long walk to clear my mind and on the way back heard Clive calling from the garden. I ran to see what had happened and found that for some strange reason Gyppo, who had been having a roll in the field, had got one of her legs caught in some wire netting and was unable to get up. Between us we managed to pull her free and to my horror I managed to twist my back. By the next morning I was in agony and so the big donkey removal was delayed until the following week. Colin Please, who had helped us in the past, arranged for his three biggest wagons to be available. Desperate phone calls to Judith Forbes brought the offer of one of their large barns which was a tremendous help as it meant all the donkeys could be in one place, isolated together whilst we had time to sort them out.

Daily conversations with Miss Jarrett or Mr Holman highlighted so many problems relating to the estate it just seemed impossible. Miss Philpin had advertised for her donkey sanctuary and donations were coming in steadily. The Charity Commission thought that long term, by amalgamating the charities, we would in fact become financially sound although in the initial stages we would have to take over all Miss Philpin's charity debts.

Every post that came seemed to bring about a little bit of bad news. A letter from the Woodley branch of Miss Philpin's bank drew my attention to the overdraft of the donkey sanctuary account and another from the post office indicated mail had been stolen in the past and they now had managed to find one of the culprits who was being prosecuted. Redundancy payments for the employees of Miss Philpin were pressing and I was having quite a job sorting out the amounts due to each man.

By the second weekend after Miss Philpin's death I felt absolutely dreadful. Our whole life had been upturned, I hardly had time to look at my own donkeys in the yard or my children or my husband and the paperwork was building up at an impossible rate. Our dear friend, Guy Thornley, had become tired of his motor boat and the three of us had bought a yacht called *Bandolier* as Niels and I had always loved sailing. So on that weekend I sailed away from it all to have forty-eight hours of relief out at sea. It was wonderful just to have some freedom and when I got back on Monday the problems could be looked at in perspective.

The biggest job was bringing the donkeys back from Reading, and what a trek it was. We left at four in the morning with the three wagons and arrived at the Reading sanctuary at half past nine; 26 July was a pouring wet cold day. As we drove down the long track into Springfield little groups of donkeys were huddled in the rain either in the shantytown shelters or under trees in the fields. At the best of times donkeys can be difficult to load, especially donkeys who have been in trouble in the past. To many of them wagons bring back memories of cruelty and terror and it took us four hours to load them up.

It was a very long journey for the donkeys and the wagons had to stop frequently so that we could make sure they were all travelling standing up and that none was in any serious trouble. At long last the wagons rolled into the large barn that Mrs Forbes was renting us. It was filled with clean straw, the racks were full of sweet hay and fresh water sparkled in the large troughs. We opened the back of the first wagon and the donkeys gratefully struggled down the ramp and into their new quarters. It was very gratifying to stand and watch them walking round the large, airy barn obviously happy to see their new surroundings, but what a mixed bunch they were. Some were obviously very young and very thin, others elderly and tired.

When the wagons had left we walked round through them all. Poor Miss Philpin, it was quite obvious that the donkeys she had taken towards the end of her life had not had the love and attention she had bestowed on them in earlier days. We had the chance now to continue her work and to carry on as we knew she had been able to do in her youth. We were just exhausted that night but grateful to know that all the donkeys were now safely in care.

We were going to clear as many of the donkey huts from the sanctuary at Reading as we could and transport them down to Ottery St Mary. Paul, who had broken up from school, and Mr Rivers who had previously worked there and his son offered to help as well. I ran Paul back up to Reading with a tent and he settled in to start the long job of clearing the site. But what had appeared sound buildings had in fact been erected many years ago and when dismantled mostly just broke to pieces and the huts were almost worthless. Paul spent three weeks on the site clearing up, lighting bonfires and generally trying to put the place back straight to comply with the stipulations laid down on the leasing of the property.

Back for a well-earned weekend's rest, having been camping out rough, he came to join the family for a sail on the Sunday on one of our precious family outings. Minutes before we were due to leave and with the picnic all packed, we heard a horrible shout from outside and found Paul lying by the gate in the yard. He had decided to vault it and as he put one hand on it to leap over, the gate clicked open with the result that he fell very heavily. He had broken his shoulder bone and all thoughts of sailing vanished for the day as we had to rush him to Exeter Orthopaedic Hospital for x-rays and to have it set. That was the end of Paul's help as far as Reading was concerned and he was in considerable pain for the next week, unable to move around at all.

The day after Paul's accident, when I was feeling particularly depressed, I was out grooming in the yard when a strange man appeared, passed an envelope to me, having ascertained that I was Mrs Svendsen, and then vanished before I had time to open it. It was the first time I had been issued with a writ and it was on behalf of Mr Light, claiming that a sum of £3,910 with reference to donkeys supplied to Miss Philpin by him was unpaid.

The letter went straight on to our lawyer, John Lovell, and between us we wrote a letter back stating that we were fully prepared to meet all the debts incurred by Miss Philpin which were substantiated but that, dealing with money that had been donated by the public, both we and the Charity Commissioners had to be fully satisfied about all claims met. Miss Philpin always paid dealers in cash apparently and the dealers refused to leave the donkeys if cash wasn't received. We pointed out that we would consider the claim when the two charities had been amalgamated.

In the post that morning I received a letter from the Charity Commission saying that the amalgamation of the two charities would be formally established on 10 September when the new trustees would become liable for all outstanding charity bills owed by Miss Philpin.

A telephone call a few moments after the writ came announced that a group of eleven donkeys was coming in from Henley. That really did a lot to cheer me up! They were some of Miss Philpin's donkeys who had been out in good homes and they proved to be some of the most unusual character donkeys we had ever had in. They arrived in extremely good condition and two of them were absolutely jet black in colour. One was Sebastian and the other Treacle. Treacle was half Sebastian's size and had a terrible hunched back. Despite that he was absolutely full of charm as far as humans were concerned and energy as far as donkeys were concerned. He ordered all the other donkeys about and from the moment he walked into the big barn at Farway he took control. If Treacle said nobody was going to eat anything until he'd had some, not one donkey would move. Even today Treacle controls a group of sixty geldings out at one of our large farms.

And it was at about this time that I first heard directly from a man I shall call Mr Bloggs. He lived near Bristol and had looked after twenty-two donkeys for about the last three years for Miss Philpin for each of which he was receiving two pounds a week for keep. He had read of Miss Philpin's death in the newspaper and was not surprised when I rang him to ask if I could come out and see the donkeys and take them back to the sanctuary. The charity owed him a great deal of money, he said, and I assured him that once we were in a position to pay we would do so. I arranged to call and see him on 8 September on my way back from Stoneleigh, where the Donkey Breed Society was holding its show.

I called in to see Mr and Mrs Bloggs at their little cottage two days before the charities were amalgamated. They were just starting Sunday lunch. We discussed the donkeys which they said were in a nearby field. I'd pick them up with the wagon the following day, I said, and they had no objections at all. Provided the donkeys were in good shape their cheque would come as soon as the amalgamation went through and the Bloggs seemed quite happy about things.

Colin Please again contracted to do the journey and he set off with his wagon to pick up the twenty-two donkeys. I was discussing my problems with Rosalind de Wesselow, who was staying with us, when the telephone rang; it was Judith Forbes. 'Betty, the wagon's just arrived, please come at once, it's absolutely terrible, I just can't believe my eyes.'

It was unlike Judith to panic. 'Whatever's the matter?' I asked. 'You should just *see* the state of these donkeys, Betty. It is absolutely appalling. *Please* come quickly.'

We jumped into the car and drove round to Farway. Two of the donkeys were in the most frightful condition I had ever seen.

We named the poor little things Hansel and Gretel. Unable to stand up unaided they were walking skeletons covered with filth and lice. The other twenty were not much better. We immediately rang the RSPCA. I was determined to make a case of these animals, particularly as the Trust had been paying two pounds a week for their care. And, for courtesy's sake, though not with a good heart, we told Mrs Bloggs of our action.

Photographs of them were taken while the RSPCA were present and then began the desperate job of starting their recovery. Hansel and Gretel had small amounts of warm bran mash and we put out hay for them before quietly leaving them in a deeply bedded box to recover from the journey. We all doubted they would be alive in the morning but peace and quiet was essential if they were to have any chance.

Mr Bloggs must have got the name of our transporter and from him Judith Forbes' phone number. He wanted the address where the donkeys were, so he could pick them up again the next day as he understood we weren't going to pay him. Panic. I advised the police who were marvellous and having seen the photographs of the donkeys stationed themselves near by. As far as we know it was just an idle threat.

Poor Hansel and Gretel. Back to Salston Close they came as soon as fit to travel, and we became extremely fond of them. I managed to clip away most of the large infected areas of hair and skin and gradually they became less terrified and more handleable as they realized that their life style had undergone a drastic change.

The case against Mr Bloggs came up on 9 December and with Niels, our veterinary surgeon and the RSPCA, all of whom were to give evidence, we arrived at the court in good time. I got so angry as I heard the evidence given in defence of Mr Bloggs about the beautiful treatment the animals had received, the veterinary care, so on and so forth. Both Mr and Mrs Bloggs were found guilty under the Protection of Animals Act, 1911, and fined the maximum penalty of £50 each.

Zebedee was our other donkey in the group who ran into problems. I called him Zebedee because he had very distinctive striped legs almost like a zebra. From the moment he came, he was extremely weak and had large ulcerous sores all over his body. The vet and Niels rigged a sling to support him as he was too weak to stand on his own and constant lying down was rubbing the ulcers which must have been extremely painful for him. Poor Zebedee had come too late, and after one last night's desperate struggle he died.

We lost three more of the group before the year was out, due to their long period of starvation and lack of care. The death of a donkey always affects me deeply, I always feel that in some way I have failed the animal and in Zebedee's case even though I had had him so short a time I felt I ought to have been able to do more for him in some way. Poor old Niels had another sleepless night trying to comfort me!

5   We find Slade House Farm

Apart from the donkeys, we had other worries. We were having an indoor swimming pool built at the hotel and we had to solve the Saturday night dinner dances problem: they were not well attended and expensive to organize. Niels decided it would be better to have an extensive *à la carte* menu. On the very first Saturday he went up to the hotel at six o'clock to make sure that everything was ready for a full evening's bookings which included a party of twenty-five officers and marines from Lympstone as well as sixty-five other bookings from parties large and small. The telephone rang in the house and Niels' anxious voice said, 'Bet, can you spare five minutes? We seem to have a problem up here.'

I ran up the hill to the hotel to find Niels standing in the main doorway. 'I can't understand it. Nothing's prepared in the kitchen at all and I've been up to Chef John's bedroom – it's all been cleaned out.' He had upped and walked out on us. And from the look on Niels' face it was quite obvious who was going to have to stand in. Not one potato was peeled, not a vegetable prepared, and even worse no meat had been taken out of the freezers or cooked off.

'How long have I got, Niels?' I asked weakly, looking round.

'About an hour,' said Niels. 'I'll try to send somebody down to help you.'

And with that he vanished, leaving me in the empty kitchen. Well, it was a complete fiasco! Niels made up the menu with the chef and I have no doubt that had he been there the duckling *à l'orange*, the chicken Kiev, and the fillet of steak *au poivre* would have been all that they sounded on the menu, but although I am a reasonable cook I think I would have needed three days to prepare everything for that evening! The final crunch came when two of the officers from Lympstone sent back the Dover soles that I had sent out. The report from a very flustered head waiter was, 'Madam, he sent them back, he says they are not Dover soles.'

'Of course they are Dover soles,' I said crossly, and pushed the two plates back at the head waiter who sent them back into the dining room once again. Within moments he reappeared with the two plates still in his hands. 'Madam, they say they've eaten all over the world and that these are definitely not Dover soles no matter what the chef in the kitchen says.'

Grimly grabbing a packet of frozen Dover soles, clearly labelled, I marched into an astonished dining room, slammed them on to the table next to the two complaining officers and said through grim lips, 'These are the Dover soles which you have had. If you want any arguments I will be pleased if you have them with Smethurst and not me,' and I then slammed back to my kitchen.

The following morning Niels managed to get a relief chef and I am pleased to say I haven't been asked to cook at the Salston again. The following day I received the results of a small advert for funds put in the *Daily Telegraph*, a magnificent post of over thirty-five letters. Niels had not gone to work when the postman came and as I sat looking at the pile of mail for the first time I began to feel extremely incompetent.

'I really can't manage Niels,' I said to him quietly. 'It has all got too much. I can cope with the donkeys and that side of it but the paperwork is just getting out of hand. I can't write thirty letters back this morning as well as groom out all these donkeys, go up to Farway and check that everything is going well and deal with all the post that I didn't have time to cope with yesterday.'

I think it was the first time I had actually broken down. 'Come on, darling, I can help you. I have got a secretary I can let you borrow this morning and then you must put an advert in and start getting your own staff. You just can't go on like this without somebody to give you some help.'

'But as soon as you start taking staff in that's when your money starts going out.'

'Well, you're just going to have to face it,' said Niels, comfortingly, 'it is going to get bigger and there is no way you can manage without getting more money in. You are just going to have to employ somebody.'

'But where can we put them?' I said. 'The house is so small, there isn't any room to have an office anywhere.'

Niels pointed through the kitchen window. 'We don't need the garage,' he said, happily. 'Let's convert the garage into an office and then you can put your girl in there with a typewriter and do all the paperwork from there.'

There and then we rang the local builder who agreed to come down and convert it into an office. As a result of our advertisement, Carol Bennett joined me and she was an extremely fast typist, managing to cope with answering great batches of letters. There were a tremendous number of legal problems in winding up the Philpin estate and a depressing number of bills that were coming in from people claiming money she had owed them during her lifetime, and in the meantime the donkeys were still coming in.

When a donkey came in, it was isolated to make sure that it wasn't suffering from any infectious disease and to give us time to give it affection. The day Gertrude arrived was the same as any other. She was extremely elderly and a very, very tired old donkey. Her breathing seemed shallow and rapid and so I rang a vet late in the afternoon to ask him if he would come out and have a look at her, and he kindly agreed to come. I thought she'd got pneumonia. By the time the vet arrived Gertrude was lying in the stable and he bent down over her to put his stethoscope to her lungs. To my complete amazement, the most peculiar thing then happened; slowly the vet collapsed on top of Gertrude and rolling slightly over lay next to her in the straw. His eyes were shut and he was breathing very heavily, certainly in comparison to Gertrude's shallow breathing. I just couldn't believe it. I stood there looking at the two of them lying there together and then shot out through the stable yelling for Herb. 'Quick, Herb, go into Gertrude's box. The vet's lying down next to her.' I rushed into the house and rang the doctor.

'I think our vet's had a heart attack. Can you come quickly? He's collapsed with a donkey.'

Luckily the doctor arrived at the stable door complete with his medical bag within five minutes. He knelt down by the vet and after a couple of moments gave me a very peculiar look. 'Herb, will you just help me and we'll carry him out of the stable. Betty, I am afraid he is going to have to lie on your couch in the lounge for a little while until he is recovered. Could you go and get it ready?'

I rushed into the house and opened all the doors wide so that they could carry the vet through. Shortly after, he was safely reposing on our couch, still unconscious and breathing heavily.

'Whatever is the matter?' I asked desperately.

'Um, well,' said the doctor, 'at a guess he has had just a little bit too much whisky, but it is nothing really to worry about. If you wait until he has recovered a little and then if you and Niels would run him home I think it will be doing him a good turn.'

The next day we approached Exeter Veterinary Hospital and appointed them as our new vets to the sanctuary! They have quite a large practice. One of the first things they did was to show me how to use a stethoscope properly and how to give injections as it was obvious that I would have to do a fair amount of work if we were not going to be involved in tremendously expensive veterinary bills. Clearly I wasn't to start any course of injections except with their authority and they would just leave me sufficient drugs for the treatment in progress and I was to ring them whenever help was needed.

They had their first emergency call within twenty-four hours when poor Matthew arrived. I was forced to tears by Matthew's condition, after a group of boys had attempted to castrate him using broken jam jars. Apparently they hadn't been caught and to the best of my knowledge they got away with their terrible deed. Matthew was a delightful donkey and despite the worst that could possibly have ever been done to him he never showed any malice or spite. I used to sit with him in the evenings sometimes and talk to him to prove to him that his faith in human nature had not been misguided.

It was extremely convenient living where we did and we had managed to buy Salston Close well from a financial point of view and only owed a small mortgage on it. The house suited us completely, it was near the children's schools and only a minute's walk away from the hotel. We spent a lot of time getting our garden nice and making friends in the neighbourhood, but there was one big problem now. It was just not big enough for us and the donkeys.

We had a family meeting and got all the children together and they took the news of an impending move extremely well. Lise and Paul were happy at school and Clive had gone to the convent school at Ottery St Mary where he had friends. We were determined to live near enough for the children to continue at their schools and to keep up their friendships but it was not going to be easy.

Carol was now struggling desperately with the post, as the donations were coming in readily and Julie Pollicut joined us in October. When Julie arrived for her interview I was doing the difficult job of clipping Gretel, who had so many sores that it was only possible to do it with scissors and Hansel wouldn't be separated from her so I was trying to keep him drinking his milk in the bucket next to hers whilst I got on with the job.

From the moment she walked into the yard Julie became an essential part of the sanctuary. Having two people to help in the office was a great relief but it seemed time to call a meeting of the trustees so that we could solve the problems that faced us together.

And we had a few to face. There were now 184 donkeys in care, with some of Miss Philpin's still to trace. The missing thirty-six donkeys reputed to be in Ireland seemed to have vanished completely as had the person who had been paid in the past. Numerous attempts got us nowhere in tracing them.

Almost immediately after a trustees' meeting at which it was agreed that we would just have to get more accommodation, the BBC rang wanting to do a follow-up story on the original Bob Forbes interview. Obviously we were pleased and they did a six-minute programme which appeared on *Spotlight*. The response was extremely good and within six days we had received £500 as a direct result and a tremendous number of offers of homes and farms for the donkeys.

At this time we heard through one of the local estate agents that a farm, Slade House, was for sale at Salcombe Regis near Sidmouth, and Niels and I went up to visit it and talked to the owners. The minute we saw it we knew it was absolutely ideal. Gentle sloping fields running down to the sea, large traditional barns which, although in poor order, could obviously be put right without too much cost. The house itself was big but we could see it would be easy to convert some of the outbuildings into offices. The biggest snag, of course, was the price.

The sum of £85,000 was a tremendous amount of money to find. John Lovell suggested that we employed a separate valuation officer who would split the property into two so that we bought the house and the ground on which it and the outbuildings stood, and the Donkey Sanctuary bought all the stable blocks and hay barns and the land. Obviously the sanctuary had not got the full amount and I just had to live where the donkeys would get the 24-hour attention they needed. The whole project was worrying. There we were happily settled and faced with a move that was going to be gigantic and plunge us deeply into debt.

Miraculously the vendor was willing to leave a first mortgage of £20,000 and by selling our own home we would just be able to manage the rest. We had committed ourselves to a family skiing holiday in January and despite pleading telephone calls we found we were unable to cancel this without paying two-thirds of the total cost. The situation for the donkeys had already become critical and it was absolutely impossible to carry on as we were.

Our beautiful little house went up for sale and the legal negotiations to purchase Slade House Farm started. With the exception of John Lovell, who had always been extremely perceptive, the response of other professional bodies when hearing that we wanted Slade House Farm for donkeys had ranged from those who considered it humorous to those who just couldn't understand why we were wasting our time on such animals. One gentleman from Sidmouth, and he'll be nameless, irritated me so much when he said, 'Fancy using such good land for donkeys. What possible use are donkeys? They are no good to anybody, they are not even any good for food, and it seems to me a sin to keep them in such a lovely area of outstanding natural beauty.'

His comments hurt me in a most peculiar way. I have never needed a reason for looking after the donkeys. After all who is to say that humans are of any more use? To me any animal or creature has as much right as another to live. But his words had sunk home. Suddenly one morning I woke Niels up at two thirty with the great shout of 'Eureka'. Poor Niels, his life wasn't easy at that moment and to be woken up by me sitting bolt upright in bed when he had just managed to get to sleep after a hard day at the hotel must have been irritating to say the least.

'Oh, what now, darling?' he asked, slightly irritated.

'Niels, I've got it, I've got it,' I said leaping up and down on the bed.

'Got what?' He was even more irritated.

'Niels, I've got the perfect use for donkeys. Why don't we put handicapped children together with donkeys? You know what the donkeys are like when these children come round. They absolutely adore them and they are so gentle. Don't you think it's possible that they can both give to each other? After all, we rescued the donkeys, how lovely if they could help and rescue the children.'

Niels sat up in bed, all thoughts of sleep having fled. 'I think it's a jolly good idea,' he said. 'It would certainly quieten any of the critics who go round saying "What use are donkeys?", but how are you going to do it?'

It was obvious Niels wasn't going to get any peace for a while and so we got up and went down into the kitchen where we made coffee and discussed different ways of setting up an organization which could bring the children and donkeys together. A new charity to handle things would obviously have to be formed as people who were supporting the Donkey Sanctuary might not like to think that any of their funds were going to help handicapped children. We were already becoming aware of how difficult some people can be! But we'd decided to find a way of making the idea work by the time we went back to bed at five o'clock. We just had to bide our time a bit.

We'd kept on the advertising agency Miss Philpin had used and Ken Birks, their director, worked out the campaign for our Christmas advertising. 'In the spirit of Christmas please throw a lifeline to help a little donkey in distress. Your donations are desperately needed' appeared in four national papers. The cost then was about £650 for each paper and while the ad ran I was on tenterhooks. The response was overwhelming, with letters pouring in at the rate of three hundred a day. Carol, Julie and I spent hours doing the receipts and the thank-you letters. With all our replies we sent a leaflet explaining the work done to date and made sure that people knew our charity was registered and that it was carrying on the work of Miss Philpin.

That Christmas really was a nightmare! Niels being of Danish descent we'd always celebrated Christmas on Christmas Eve. In between answering the post and telephone calls there was only just time to prepare our traditional goose which was stuffed with apples and prunes and to make the rice pudding, in which one almond only is placed and whoever finds it wins a box of chocolates. The evening started with the large dinner at six thirty because the children just couldn't wait any longer and the first excitement of course was the rice pudding to find the lucky almond. We always had both sets of grannies and grandpas down and even they got excited as the evening went on.

Leaving the grandparents in charge after dinner, Niels and I slipped over to the hotel where there was Christmas Eve Danish Style for the guests, including the 'lucky almond' in the rice pudding. Niels announced to the 150 guests that the one who found the lucky almond would receive a two-pound box of Black Magic. However, within seconds the smile began to fade from his face as in turn hands began going up all over the room. 'Here, we have the almond, we have the almond,' echoed from all round the room. Frantically Niels rushed into the kitchen. 'Chef, what have you done?' he asked. 'I said just one almond in the pudding.' The chef smiled happily at Niels. 'Oh, you couldn't just put one almond in, Mr Svendsen, it wouldn't taste at all. I shook the whole bag in.' Niels had to raid the bar to find some spare boxes of chocolates and bang went all the profit from the Christmas dinner!

The purchase of Slade Farm seemed to be going quite smoothly but just before we left on our skiing holiday I received a bombshell in the form of a letter from the planning authorities. Allowing donkeys on Slade House Farm, Salcombe Regis, instead of cows and sheep, constituted a change of use and we would need planning permission for it to be used as a donkey sanctuary. By this time we had a buyer for our house, and we were terrified that if we delayed everything would fall through. It was a terrible time to have to go away on holiday and there is no doubt that the first few days were marred by the worry of what was happening at home. But on the sixth day we received a telephone call from the hotel to tell us that East Devon District Council's planning committee had agreed to change the use of the farm to a donkey sanctuary and allow us to create an office there.

Lise was by now doing a course at the same college in London that I had attended and I really missed her. It seemed a good idea to combine a visit to Ken Birks at the agency with seeing Lise, and Ken kindly offered to take us both to a casino in the West End. After a delicious dinner at which Lise had three different creamy puddings, we went down to the tables to try our hand at roulette. Once, years ago, when Niels and I were on holiday in Tunisia, I'd actually managed to win £36 on a two-shilling bet.

Anyway there we sat, me feeling thrilled with my small pile of chips and Ken enjoying watching us having fun, when I glanced at Lise; she'd gone white as a sheet, and was sweating freely. Suddenly she dived out of the casino and I had no option but to follow. The chips went back to Ken, sadly, and Lise had to spend the night in my hotel room being violently sick. She was too ill to go back to the college. It was those puddings.

The most vitriolic letter from a man I'll call Percy awaited my return. In a nutshell he claimed our advertising was designed to make gullible elderly people part with their money and that the whole of the Donkey Sanctuary was a façade whose purpose was to collect funds from the public for my husband and me to be able to enjoy ourselves and to run big cars and to subsidize our hotel! His final sentence threatened letters to the *Telegraph* and *The Times* to expose our charity. I was, to say the least, worried. I decided to ring the Charity Commission to get their advice on this type of letter. To my amazement the commissioner roared with laughter when he heard who had written the letter and said, 'Oh, you've got Percy now. I think every other charity in the country gets a letter from Percy at regular intervals. Just throw it in the wastepaper basket.'

That afternoon, Niels was sitting quietly working in his office at the hotel when an immaculate Rolls-Royce pulled up outside his window and the chauffeur got out.

By the time Niels got to the front door, the beautiful Rolls was driving slowly down the lane towards our house. He rushed to the receptionist and said, 'Who was it, Who was it? Are they coming to stay?' Only to be told, 'No, I am sorry, Mr Svendsen. They've just come to visit the sanctuary.'

I was equally startled to see the Rolls glide into our little private yard and by the time I had got outside even more surprised to find an elderly lady chopping up carrots on the immaculate car bonnet for our donkeys. Having seen how the rescued donkeys were getting along and fed them the carrots, she gave us a cheque for £100 and went on her way!

A letter came from James Mason. Julie and I read it carefully and turned it over and discussed it. The postmark was from Switzerland and finally when writing to acknowledge the cheque I put the words at the bottom – 'Are you possibly *the* James Mason?' The letter came back by return – 'Yes, I am *the* James Mason and am delighted and heartened by the work that you are doing.' Later he became a patron of the Slade Centre.

Planning the great move to Slade House Farm was under way. The house needed a great deal of work and we decided we would live in one of the flats above the outbuildings next to the house. It had two minute bedrooms, a minute dining room/lounge and a kitchen. The total area was approximately 240 square feet, and to get our large family in was quite a feat!

Before we could move the donkeys' fencing had to be put up in the new farm and I contacted one of the big fencing firms and their representative came up to see me. We went all round the farm property together working out where the fences would go to give us the maximum number of fields with approximately five acres in each. A proportion of the property consisted of a woodland area and if fenced carefully the donkeys could enjoy the odd forage through the woods, obtaining many kinds of trace minerals from the various tree barks. The slope in places was almost vertical and Mr Benton and I spent a very difficult four hours covering every inch of the boundary, clambering and scrambling up banks. He was exhausted by the time we returned to the farm and I didn't feel all that much better.

A small firm of local contractors started getting the stable blocks into order and made the long cow shed into five individual boxes, with a walk along the back so that we could feed the hay into racks and the food and water into troughs without having to actually enter each stable. There was a tremendous air of activity all round the farm area.

Herb Fry's son, John, had a good agricultural training and had been working for some years with a large local farmer in a neighbouring village, and knowing Herb's excellent qualities I decided to have a chat with John before I appointed any staff for Slade. He was a typical young Devonshire farmer – tall, well built and full of fun. We immediately liked each other and he struck me as the ideal person for the practical side of the donkey work. He agreed to join us and with his wife, Monica, moved into the three-bedroomed house that we had bought with the farm property. We walked right round the farm discussing plans. One field at the far end of the farm was in very poor shape and we both stood there looking at it, when John suddenly turned to me and said, 'I suggest rape in here – it would be just the thing.' I must confess slight hesitation on my part. After all I had only just met him and we were quite out of earshot of anyone else. He turned and saw me looking anxious. 'I do mean the crop,' he said quickly.

Every field needed its own shelter and so another trustees' meeting had to approve the fencing which was going to cost £6,500 and the building of a £600 shelter in each field. We certainly did not have sufficient funds to meet the bill! As usual I was relying on my guardian angel to produce a miracle but fields without shelters were no use to our poor old donkeys. The day of the great move came and, with all our furniture in storage, Niels and I and the children moved into the tiny flat on 28 February 1975. The old Aga was being taken out of the farm kitchen, all the floor boards were up everywhere as the pipes were leaking and we took the opportunity to put central heating in since the house felt extremely cold and was in a very exposed position. It was chaos but all exciting, adventurous and new.

The donkey move was very much easier than we thought it would be. Even the very old and sick ones managed well and it was surprising how they tackled the journey, quite obviously enjoying their new quarters on arrival. We had now taken 232 donkeys into care.

Our first visitor in the tiny flat was a reporter from the *Daily Mirror*. We were all sitting having tea when there was a knock at the door and a head appeared round the doorway. 'Did you know you had been left a legacy of £6,000?' he announced tersely.

'No,' said everybody, putting down knives and forks. He came into the room. 'Well, you have. It is from a man in Pontypool, surely you have heard of him?'

'Never heard a thing,' we all said truthfully.

This particular gentleman had always been teased and called a donkey by his friends; to the absolute horror of all his relatives on his death his will quite clearly stated that, because of this, donkeys should get all his money; everything he possessed was to go to the Donkey Sanctuary in Devon. Was my luck tailored to fit the fencing bill? I wondered.

It seemed, on reflection, that all the experiences of my life had been leading up to my being able to cope with my current situation. My love of animals and children must have been born with me, and I had ample business experience with my father's works and Modeq. Working with the donkeys every day and getting to know them well as I did helped to build up my knowledge of their needs. Walking into a field and looking round the donkeys to see the way they were breathing, walking, or even standing, I could assess their general health and if they were feeling off colour; indeed, many of them would come up and tell me as they had grown so used to me by now.

A number of the donkeys we received were stallions. Because they were 'entire', as they are known in the trade, they brought many problems to a sanctuary. We had enough donkeys without breeding any more! They are also much noisier and more difficult to handle than geldings and can be quite bad-tempered. All had to be gelded, quite a costly operation, but once gelded they become gentle and placid and can settle down to a quiet community life. Unfortunately many of the mares arrived already in foal and foaling down some of these donkeys could be difficult. We would never know the proper date the foal was expected and would spend night after night going round the stables to make sure that they hadn't gone into labour with none of us there to help if problems arose.

A beautiful gentle donkey called Beatrice came in just after we moved into the new house. I was called out to the new stables by the donkeys' braying, which is their usual way of letting me know they need attention, to find the dearest little foal, which we

87

called Tulip Time, had been born. She was the deepest chocolate colour I have ever seen and absolutely covered with a long shaggy coat which almost reached her dear little hooves. It still does grow enormously fast and Tulip Time has been a great joy to all of us.

By now I had completely stopped breeding donkeys and my lovely stallion St Paddy had been gelded. A Donkey Breed Society member could no longer keep her stud and I did eventually agree to take her tribe after first pointing out any stallions would have to be gelded.

'You're not going to like what you see, Mrs Svendsen,' said the driver, when they arrived. 'They look all right but they don't seem to be walking properly, although their feet aren't too bad.'

The back of the box came down and a row of anxious eyes and twitching ears met me. But there was something not quite right. Slowly they came down the ramp and stood in the yard. One of them obviously had tremendous difficulty with walking. We decided to put them in their boxes for the night and get the vet next morning.

Now, in the trade, cake is another name given for the hard feed given to the animals. Usually it consists of horse or pony cubes or animal stock cubes which are a mixture of dried grass and nutritive additives and the owner of the stud had sent a load of cake in with the donkeys. The driver struggled out with the big tea chests. I took the top cover idly off the one that I had helped him with. All I could see was clear plastic wrapping paper. To our horror we uncovered layer upon layer of confectionery cakes ranging from battenburgs and chocolate cakes to ginger cakes. All types – each box was full. We were absolutely amazed and stood looking at each other.

I went indoors and rang the lady who had sent them in. 'Oh yes, dear, you got the cake?' she said brightly. 'Um, yes.' I said. 'Why that sort of cake in particular?' 'Well, dear, we live next door to a baker and they let us have as much as we like free and it says in all the books feed them on cake so this is what they have been living on!'

The vet confirmed my worst fears and our hearts sank as we examined each donkey. Bilko had severe rickets and her mother,

My Poppett, who was in fact only three years old herself, was heavily in foal yet again.

'We are going to have a real struggle with these,' said the vet. 'It's going to take years to get them right.'

They all had to be put on to a special diet which included Abidec daily and Cytacon syrup added to their bran mash with black treacle. Slowly the condition of the donkeys improved. The driver who'd brought them in was David Home. He had recently joined John Fry in the yard and was wonderful with animals.

At long last the new office was ready and the staff who'd still been at Salston Close moved. We also brought up the safe and the men levered it carefully into position whereupon it slowly sank out of sight! Obviously it was far too heavy for the floor, and there was a hilarious half hour while they worked out how to drag it back up again. It gave Niels and me some very much needed light relief.

Very shortly after the arrival of My Poppett and family another sad case came in. We had received a letter from a Mrs Bunday asking us if we could take in a donkey that she said she had rescued from an Animal Research Station. Apparently they sell donkeys and ponies after they have finished their research work on them. Mrs Bunday saw Mollie and decided to buy her at once. She had been used for womb transplant purposes and Mrs Bunday had had her for a short while. However, the field she had been promised in which to keep Mollie had not been available and she felt that perhaps we could take her and give her a good retirement.

Dear Mollie Bunday, she was well over thirty, and how anyone could have expected a transplant to work on a mare of this age was impossible to understand. She was far too quiet to be healthy, in addition to which she was suffering from arthritis and was broken winded, her teeth were in bad need of attention and she couldn't even manage to chew hay properly. My heart nearly broke with hers. We loved her and we cossetted her and gradually she began to improve a little. She settled down very well with My Poppett's group, especially with Fuzzy, one of the very older donkeys from that group who had bad feet and who moved very slowly and quietly as well.

Our youngest daughter, Sarah, was still having a lot of problems with her eyes and she had already had one operation but the next was going to be a little more serious. The sister at the hospital sent me off home quite firmly. 'Now I don't want to see you again, Mrs Svendsen, until I phone you at eleven or twelve o'clock when it will all be nicely over, won't it?' she said, smiling brightly at Sarah who was lying somewhat miserably in bed.

I said goodbye, trying to be brave, but outside in the corridor I asked the sister, 'Please let me be here when she comes back from the theatre. I would much rather be near at hand in case she needs me.'

'Now, Mrs Svendsen,' she said. 'Don't fuss. I've dealt with children all my life and they are much better without their mothers hanging about. I will ring you when we need you.'

Julie brought me interminable cups of coffee next morning until suddenly the telephone rang. It was half past ten. As I picked it up I recognized the shrill screaming in the background. 'Mrs Svendsen, can you get in as quickly as possible?' said the sister. 'Your daughter seems to require you,' and the phone went dead.

I belted into Exeter and as I walked into the hospital through its large front door I could hear the screams in the distance. One thing Sarah has always had if not good eyes and that is good lungs and she was certainly exercising them. Her poor little face was all swollen and a bandage completely covered both her eyes. 'Mummy, Mummy, is that you?' she whimpered but as soon as I said, 'Yes, I'm here, Sarah,' a slight smile broke out over her face and we didn't hear another word from her for over an hour. Apparently Sarah was resistant to most normal anaesthetics and the surgeon who operated on her told me it was the first time in his life a child had ever sat up before the end of an operation fully conscious on the operating table. No wonder she was hysterical for some hours after. It was lovely to get her back home again and be able to spoil her. One of the good things about the sanctuary is that I am always somewhere near at hand for the children.

Judith Forbes was getting a little bit desperate out at Farway by this time. The original numbers she offered to take had been doubled almost to one hundred and the large grazing area put aside for them at the top of her farm, which had previously been full of beautiful gorse bushes, now appeared to be a barren waste. She could no longer cope. Once the fencing and building were complete at Slade Farm, the Farway donkeys returned to the fold. As it was only approximately three miles away it seemed a good idea to walk the donkeys over rather than put them to the terrible stress of being loaded in the wagons and being driven. The *Sidmouth Herald* thought the idea of advertising for people to help walk the donkeys over was marvellous and ran the piece for people to telephone us if willing to spare the Sunday to help. The reporter, Nick Stephen, came with his friend, Heather Case, and a photographer from the *Sidmouth Herald*, and the paper promised to do us a good write-up.

Soon it became apparent that we were going to have at least two people to handle each donkey! On reflection this seemed quite a good idea as many of the donkeys had never been handled before, and along the country lanes and the short stretch of main road to the farm there could possibly be difficulties. Spillers Feeds, who had been supplying us with all our hard feed, agreed to put a watering and feeding station halfway along the route and the local girl guides agreed to act as runners in case of problems *en route*.

A car flotilla was organized by my father to drive the helpers back to Farway after the donkeys had come safely to Slade House Farm. As the *Sidmouth Herald* put it in an article entitled 'Gid along, little donkey, gid along':

Howdy, pardners! Snowball's the name. I'm the one with the straw hat and the long floppy ears. And I'd like to tell you about the best dog-gone thing that's hit the West since bangers and beans.

I'm talking about the great donkey drive on Sunday when hundreds of folks moved me and my buddies from Farway Countryside Park to Slade House Farm, near Sidmouth.

Mrs Elisabeth Svendsen, the boss of the Big S ranch, reckoned she needed a bigger spread for her Donkey Sanctuary.

So she up and sold her old homestead and put the money into buying a great new place at Salcombe Regis.

Once she'd taken over the new range, she had herself a powerful headache – how to get me and the other 100 in the herd up there.

Sure, she could have used the wagon, but, come sundown, she'd had been plumb tuckered out. And half of the herd would have been at Salcombe whilst the other half would be at Farway.

Then she had a great idea. Hire some drovers from outside, and let them move the herd on foot.

So on Sunday we were all rounded up into the corral. Crowds of people were there. There were the drivers, the Girl Guide helpers and some men from that new-fangled thing they call television. One by one we moved out and set off across the prairies of East Devon.

I was one of the first to get going – with my two drovers, Heather Case and Nick Stephen, from the good old *Sidmouth Herald*.

The plan was to move the herd a couple of miles to the Long Chimney ranch and stop for some chow. Then we'd set off again so we would be at the new ranch by high noon.

Now, as some of you good folks probably know, donkeys can be mean, stubborn critters when they want to be.

I'm a good donkey myself and I don't give any trouble. But when I saw some of my buddies . . . well, it made me feel ashamed. Some of them kept stopping to eat grass. Then they charged off, dragging the poor old drovers along with them. A couple of times I was sure there was going to be a stampede.

Then there were the real awkward ones. They just dug their heels in and refused to move. I pitied one or two of the drovers. As you can see from the pictures, you can't make a donkey go where he don't wanna go.

One or two of the drovers got so bushed they just plumb gave in and they and the donkeys were picked up in the wagon. And although 1,000 people volunteered to be drovers on the day, there weren't quite enough to go round and a few of the donkeys had to travel all the way in the wagon.

But most of us kept going on foot. When we got to the main Sidmouth–Lyme stagecoach route we were a bit worried in case we got mixed up with the wagon trains that were passing through.

We needn't have worried. The local lawman, Marshal Holsgrove, was on hand with a posse of men from the Sidmouth sheriff's office, and all went smoothly.

We made good time to the Donkey Sanctuary – in fact, although it took about three hours, it seemed so quick that you only had time to say 'Jiminy Cricket' before we were there.

'Course, Ma Svendsen had to be at the Donkey Sanctuary ranch to greet everyone, so she went on ahead in the chuck wagon. Later on some of the drovers got a ride back to Farway in the buggy.

Meanwhile, we were turned out into the corral, where we've got us some smart new bunkhouses. I can tell you, when we hit the hay on Sunday night, we all slept real well.

Well, folks, that's the end of my story. Except for one thing, Mrs Svendsen and me would like to thank all you folks who came and helped in the donkey drive on Sunday. It was mighty kind of you. Yep, mighty kind.

No longer working full time in the hotel I had had to forgo my salary there and obviously, as a trustee, I couldn't take anything from the Donkey Sanctuary so I was hopeful that there would be some income to be drawn from the twelve caravans in a field we'd bought with the house, and from three flats above what was being converted into our offices. But within a month of starting to convert the stables it became apparent (yet again) that we just were not going to have sufficient room for all the donkeys. One way out was to convert the previous cowshed into a barn. There was already a very poor wooden floor there but the contractors came in and had a look at the flooring upstairs and advised me that it would have to be completely redone with stressed concrete to take the weight of some thirty donkeys. The farm is on sloping ground, hence the barn with two levels.

A member of the Charity Commission happened to make a visit the day after the contractors came, and I took him out to see the barn.

'Do you really need a new floor, Mrs Svendsen?' he asked, walking round some of the hay that was stored there; then to my

horror he gave a yell as both feet began to go through the rotting boards. Perhaps it was essential after all, he agreed.

My hopes of an income from the flats were to be dashed. Getting staff was extremely difficult as the farm is well off the beaten track; frequently very good people would apply for jobs but only if we could supply accommodation; and so, one by one, the flats had to become staff flats, and of course bang went the large summer letting fees.

From the time that the first donkeys came in I had always kept a proper record sheet for each animal. Many of the donkeys arrived nameless and I got a great deal of pleasure from choosing a name that I thought would suit the animal, such as Gyppo who had come in from the gypsies. Tiny Titch and So Shy and, of course, all the donkeys from Miss Philpin had had to be identified in some way. Halters had seemed a good idea to start with and we had ordered sufficient for our first fifty donkeys, with small discs rather like those on dog collars with the donkey's name and number engraved on. This worked efficiently for the old and sick donkeys but two naughty little donkeys like Bill and Ben would get the greatest pleasure from dragging each other round by their head collars day after day; soon they started adding other donkeys to their game and I would go out in the morning to find two or three standing happily in the field with the torn remnants of halters round their necks, totally unidentifiable. Obviously when the donkeys were few in number this was all right but as we grew in size it became a problem to solve.

The farmers' view that the easiest way was to put a tag through the donkey's ear as in cattle was unacceptable, as donkeys are extremely sensitive around their ears (despite their size!) and generally hate them even being touched. Freeze-branding was suggested and we did try this on four of the earliest donkeys. The idea was that a number was branded on by an implement which was so far below freezing that the donkey felt no pain but it changed the pigmentation of the skin so that the hair would grow out white. It may work on cattle but it certainly doesn't on donkeys. Nor was I happy at their expressions during the branding. Within two months George, a chocolate colour, was the only donkey where a number could be seen, the white and the grey donkeys just healed up and grew more grey or white hair; so that was no use.

Finally, while passing a field of cows, I saw each one had a plastic collar round its neck with a number on. A bit of snooping gave me the name of the firm that made the collars and they sent twenty on trial. At last we'd found something that worked. To begin with they came with the name and number of the donkey already printed, but now, because of our large demand, we use a special type of electrically heated marking pen which melts the plastic sufficiently for the black ink placed in later to be permanent. So we can identify all our inmates and then look up their records if need be.

Naming all the donkeys taken in from Miss Philpin's sanctuary was awful. Faced with a group of over eighty it took us three days to do a full medical inspection of each one and to write up their records with all the details. Some names came quite easily. The tall grey donkey was Lofty and a very prim-looking little donkey became Gertrude. Eventually I did revert back to Fred, George, Neddy and so on as the third day drew to a close.

One of our biggest problems with large numbers of donkeys arriving was parasites; so each received a worm dose. All donkeys have parasites to a greater or lesser degree and these have to be controlled regularly otherwise a large proportion of the food that we feed in at one end is taken by the parasites. The fencing had been done to give us individual five-acre pastures so that each one could be rested at regular intervals to let the grass grow – but, more important, to kill off the parasites passed on from the donkey droppings and prevent them from being re-circulated.

We had sufficient donkeys to need them grouped. There were the stallions, awaiting castration and needing to be kept away from all the other donkeys, mares with foals which we named the nursery group, a group of new geldings which were extremely lively and spent most of the day playing with each other and galloping round the field; and then the geriatrics, which always arouse a deal of interest. We class a donkey as a geriatric when it reaches the age of thirty. Ageing them is difficult. It takes years of practice, but one key is similar to the horse in that the teeth

Niels and I with one of the
original nappy driers in the
background and Lise and Paul
(Douglas Allen)

At the height of Modeq success,
with the new factory built with
the help of the Get Ahead prize
(*Daily Mirror*)

Hansel and Gretel on arrival, and

after they had been at the Sanctuary for nine months (Nicholas Toyne, Newton Abbott)

A family of
helpers on the
great donkey trek
from Farway to
Slade House Farm

My daughter,
Lise, with Bambi
and Supremo

Bilko, one of the donkeys fed on 'cake' on arrival

(*opposite*) Twiggy, after she had been with us a while

The geriatric unit having supper

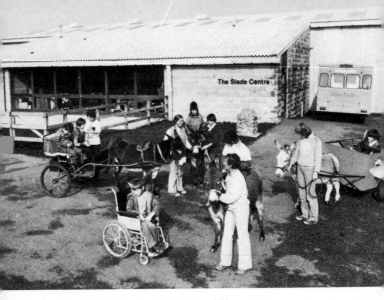

The Slade Centre, opened in 1978

The demonstration we staged outside the council offices to get the planning permission through

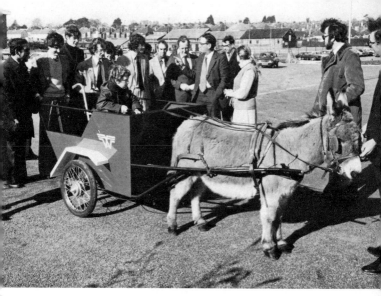

The specially built trap to carry handicapped children

A recent picture of some of our staff at Herb's retirement party

Timothy

Working on an IDPS trip in Peru

are the main indicator. With a donkey the top teeth, instead of growing longer and longer as the age of the donkey increases, wear right back until sometimes we have a donkey with an enormously long lower set of teeth with the top set right down to the gums.

In addition, the hooves give an indication, as does the general conformation and condition of the body. We know that donkeys can live until they are fifty years old and we have had donkeys who have reached this age and even passed it. A problem with the geriatrics is always to decide when it is kinder to put them down than to keep them alive.

I watch my donkeys in the geriatric ward for many, many hours and I can only say that having spent a whole lifetime working for man, reaching sanctuary gives them their first taste of freedom. I have seen donkeys coming exhausted, broken in spirit, able only to stand quietly in the corner with their head drooping, and just pleased to be able to rest for a while. The same donkeys after two months in the sanctuary are almost unrecognizable, gradually realizing they aren't going to be mistreated or have to go out to work on the beaches again and that the food comes often and regularly. But there are those cases where the cruelty and mistreatment have gone too far. Where we find an elderly donkey spending more of the day lying down than standing up then a decision has to be taken. They get what can only be termed bedsores from lying down too much; once these begin to ulcerate we call the vets, and if we consider the donkey is suffering and has no future hope then our poor old friend is humanely put down. It is always done here on our own premises and before the event the donkeys are always given ginger nuts, which they absolutely adore, and we are always with them when their final moments come.

We decided to evolve a 'donkey charter'. This grants to every donkey admitted to the sanctuary the right to life, regardless of age or health, and the best possible treatment, care and drugs to preserve its life to the maximum. It grants permanent peace and freedom, the care and protection of the sanctuary and the right to return if rehabilitated to a new home. When the time comes, it grants a dignified, peaceful death, this only being induced in the event of extreme suffering as agreed by both the veterinary advisers and sanctuary staff.

We also set up an intensive care unit. This, as its name implies, is where the donkeys are under constant medical veterinary and farrier's care every single day and it is an area split into small units, each one supplied with its own infra-red lamp; two are specifically fitted out with slings so that in the event of a donkey being temporarily unable to stand unaided we can support it during the time of its treatment to prevent it getting ulcerated sores. Donkeys such as Gyppo and Hansel and Gretel would be permanent members of such a unit.

Each unit of donkeys was given two areas, adjoining each other, in which to roam and graze. By careful planning John and I arranged it so that two groups of donkeys could never talk to each other over the hedge. This was to avoid the danger of infection from one group to another and to prevent diseases developing between the animals. This was to prove absolutely invaluable when equine flu hit the sanctuary.

Until that time, we always assumed that a three-week isolation period would be long enough, but how wrong we were. The group of twelve donkeys fed on cake did their three weeks in isolation and were then moved out into the nursery unit as many of the mares were in foal. Bilko and My Poppett went into the intensive care unit. Three days later I noticed that one of the donkeys, called Fuzzy, had developed a very bad mucus discharge from the nose. Her breathing was very rapid and I didn't like her general appearance at all. She was standing very quietly and had sweated up slightly. I called the vets who put her back into the isolation unit straight away. By next morning, however, two more of the donkeys from the group of twelve were in trouble, including My Poppett. Immediate treatment by antibiotic was essential and we started the first injection of Penbritin that day. The next day came confirmation of the ghastly news.

It was a real disaster. Amongst all my old and sick donkeys, there were many who were totally incapable of surviving such an attack and speed in sorting out those donkeys who could be infected was essential. Everybody rallied round, Niels, the children and Julie from the office. Fortunately none of the animals had been allowed into the fields but all the intensive care units were isolated as was the whole of the nursery group. In this little group was a donkey that we all love particularly. Dawlish Infant School had been to visit the sanctuary on the day that one of the rescued donkeys from Miss Philpin's sanctuary, Chippy, had produced a little foal. To make things more interesting and to get the children involved with the sanctuary we had suggested that they should name the foal and the school rang me a week later to say that they had asked every child to put a name on a piece of paper and put it into a ballot box.

They had then chosen the name which was most popular. To everybody's amazement this turned out to be John. We already had one John, and so he became Johnny Dawlish. To our horror Johnny was one of the first little foals to be affected and he died. The very day after, the school was due to visit and this left the sanctuary with a tremendous problem. We did have other little foals so would it be kinder to the children to hide the truth?

We discussed it with the school and decided that it was probably better that they accepted that Johnny Dawlish had died. The coach arrived and the children got out very quietly; their teaching staff had already told them what had happened and we held a little remembrance service for Johnny. I was heartbroken. I was already upset at losing Johnny, and the sight of all those little faces was almost more than I could bear. The children decided to adopt Chippy, his mother, in Johnny's place.

We fought the flu for a further three weeks, an immense work-load as each donkey had to be examined each day for the first sign of infection. My stethoscope proved invaluable. The first sign was an increased respiration rate and this enabled us to save the lives of many of our donkeys. That no two groups of donkeys met proved the saving of the situation. We lost two donkeys including Johnny Dawlish and my darling Peanuts, but everybody else recovered. Thereafter we decided that, despite the cost which was approximately five pounds per donkey, we would inoculate every newcomer against equine flu and that the isolation period should be extended to four weeks. The anti-flu injection also included an anti-tetanus dose and this we also welcomed as there was always fear of tetanus where such a large number of donkeys were gathered together.

The donkeys' day starts with the clattering of buckets in the feed house at 8 a.m. All the donkeys receive a breakfast equivalent of a cupped handful of low-protein pony nuts. Unlike ponies, donkeys do not need much protein and an excess can actually poison them. After breakfast the donkeys have unlimited amounts of sweet hay and those fit and out in the field units spend the rest of the day happily grazing in the fields.

Then I do the donkey rounds of all those in intensive care and they are thoroughly checked to make sure no new symptoms have developed. Those needing injections are rewarded with a ginger biscuit if they stand quietly. The farrier comes at frequent intervals, as many of those in intensive care have the most appalling hoof problems. Particularly bad cases are the donkeys left in orchards untended since ponies have taken their place, and those coming in after doing the rounds of the markets. Some are so severe as to need almost daily paring. Our farrier, John Craddock, is an extremely kind and skilled man and he takes infinite care over even the very old ones' feet.

After their treatment they are allowed out to graze for the day in the Home Paddock, which runs down from the intensive care block. Any sign of rain and back they come. Those very sick, of course, have to stay inside under the warmth of the infra-red lamp. Cold nights mean woollen rugs for many of the sick ones as this enables them to use their restricted energy on getting themselves fit rather than in keeping themselves warm.

The evening meal is always a great delight to the donkeys. It consists of bran, flaked maize, crushed oats, molasses (a form of black treacle) dampened down with a liquid made up of cows' milk, warm water and Cytacon syrup, which has a vitamin and calcium additive. Where there are more than two donkeys in a box separate feeding troughs are given to make sure that each donkey gets the right amount. The sight of the old and sick donkeys enjoying their food and happy makes me realize it's all worth while.

As with humans, illness doesn't just strike during the day and

I never cease to be amazed at the donkeys' intelligence in calling for help at night. Naughty Face, who had joined the sanctuary group, was always kept within range of my window and she sensed immediately if anyone was in trouble anywhere on the sanctuary. I strongly believe that donkeys convey messages to each other. Certainly when Naughty Face set off in the middle of the night we would always find something wrong, even if it was in the furthest field away from the sanctuary. She was an extremely intelligent donkey who, when she saw trouble, never stopped braying until the lights came on in our bedroom, which she could see from her stable. There were innumerable instances of this warning behaviour, the most usual being a donkey who had collapsed in the stable and was struggling desperately to get back up on its feet.

One particular night there was a tremendous storm blowing when Naughty Face began her bray. Niels insisted on coming with me, for which I was extremely grateful. We looked into every intensive care box and nobody was in trouble. The only donkeys still braying were in the field that stretched almost down to the sea. With our big storm torch we trudged down across the field and there, with all the donkeys in a little circle around her watching with great interest, stood Beth, one of the mares that had come from Miss Philpin, and on the ground beside her was a tiny foal. Niels picked the little foal up in his arms and carried it back to the intensive care unit. Beth followed us there. We named the foal Storm for obvious reasons, and standing looking at Beth enjoying the hot mash I had made for her, and the little foal suckling for the first time, more than made up for our disturbed night.

Gyppo had recovered sufficiently to go out into the field every day and was obviously enjoying her life very much at Slade House Farm. However, she seemed to be slowing down, and one day as David was bringing them back into the intensive care unit for their feed Gyppo lay down in the yard. She wouldn't get up and I was surprised to see David lying down on the ground next to Gyppo.

'I thought she might get up when I got up,' said David, 'if I lay down like this.'

'What a good idea,' I said, because we all hate the ignominy of pushing and pulling donkeys.

I lay down on the other side of Gyppo and after a few moments both David and I slowly stood up together. To our joy Gyppo stood up with us and very slowly walked into her box. But that night Gyppo, instead of attacking the hay rack with her usual gusto, was standing quietly in the corner with her eyes half shut. I talked to her gently for a few moments but she didn't respond and I went to bed feeling slightly worried. The following morning David gave me the very sad news that Gyppo had passed away quietly in the night. For once none of the donkeys had 'told' me. I think they all realized that her time had come and that she died a peaceful, dignified death; which of us could ask for more?

Several of the new arrivals at this time had been rescued from markets by members of the public as they were convinced that donkeys were on their way to be slaughtered for salami or pet food. The sanctuary never purchases a donkey as this could create a market similar to that made by Miss Philpin. Amongst Miss Philpin's papers I found a letter from a salami making company, which confirmed worries that many of the donkeys were in fact condemned to this fate when bought by dealers in markets. What was retrieved from Miss Philpin's files went as follows:

Mr Philpin
The Donkey Sanctuary
'Springfield'
Fosters Lane
Woodley
Berks   7 October 1972

Dear Mr Philpin
I am prompted by your advertisement in today's *Guardian* to write to you with what I hope will be a mutually beneficial business proposition.

I am the British representative of an Italian-owned company who are experiencing supply difficulties in obtaining a continuing supply of donkeys – one of the principal ingredients of salami.

My company has authorized me to offer to purchase all the donkeys currently in your care and all you manage to acquire in the future. We are particularly interested in British animals as the standard of care during their lives tends to render their flesh most suitable for the salami-producing process.

You would be in a most fortunate position to make a profit because one of our lorries would call at monthly intervals, thus relieving you of all the expenses associated with transportation, etc. At the same time you would have our assurance that these animals would be reasonably humanely destroyed on arrival in Italy whilst helping to alleviate the food production problems already emerging in Europe.

May I look forward to hearing from you in the very near future? Yours faithfully,

At this time, purely by accident, one of the visitors in the hotel who came from Essex had been involved in the donkey meat trade and I gleaned a great deal of information from him which proved conclusively to me that this exporting of donkeys was going on. They were quite good for meat as there was two and a half per cent bone-to-weight ratio. The average weight exported stood at 350 pounds per donkey. They had found that the weight loss on young or middle-aged donkeys per journey was approximately 30 pounds, an old donkey travelling had a weight loss as low as two and a half pounds. The donkeys were sent via an East Anglian shipper. At the slaughterhouse, the head, neck and lower legs were discarded as waste. At that time, transport costs to Italy, the main importers, were too high, and Germany was taking a limited supply. The price was 10p per pound less two and a half per cent bone of the net carcass weight. These factual details had horrified me despite contrary information from Ministry records.

I have to accept the fact that animals are brought up in captivity and slaughtered to provide food for humans, and this is what every farmer is in effect doing. But in accepting it I hope that the animals are reared in the best possible conditions and slaughtered the most humane way possible to prevent suffering. Following these lines, I would accept that there could be a case for using donkeys for salami; but to take half-starved, ill-treated and terrified donkeys and to put them through the ordeal of shipment abroad to face the methods of slaughter which are sometimes employed on the Continent seems cruel to me.

Amelia was exactly the colour of a child's rocking-horse, a beautiful dapple grey. She had the most terrible feet you can imagine when she arrived and was unable to stand firmly on any of her hooves. They were bent and twisted out of recognition, and as she stood she would rock gently backwards and forwards. John Craddock, our farrier, spent hours with her and eventually we did get her so that she could move around without discomfort. She spent hours nuzzling Suey, who had come in from a beach in the north of England. Some beach operators are extremely good and concerned over their animals but this had not been Suey's fortune. She had collapsed on the beach. A bystander telephoned us about this unconscious donkey lying there and mentioned a vet had been called and considered the donkey had had a heart attack. It was a long way away but we arranged with the owner to pick the donkey up and David went off in the new wagon which we had purchased specially for the job. It had padded sides so if need be we could transport a donkey standing up, supported by special slings.

It was a tiring journey for Suey. She arrived back carefully supported but with her eyes tight shut.

'She hasn't moved since I set off. She's had a little water but just keeps her eyes shut all the time and obviously takes no interest at all in her surroundings,' said David.

Her eyes were still tight shut as I stroked her gently on the nose. 'It's all right, Suey, you've arrived,' I said. 'There's no need to worry any more. Come on now, old lady, let's get you off the box.'

We undid the slings and she stood shakily without attempting to move. Whenever the box arrived in the yard all the donkeys used to put their heads out through the door to see who had come, and they were becoming impatient – a great bray came from almost every stable. Slowly Suey's eyes opened and I found myself looking into the saddest pair of eyes I had ever seen.

'Come on, Suey,' I urged. 'It's all right, you're not going to have to work any more. Your only job now is to get yourself fit and well.'

She seemed to give herself a little shake and then slowly she began to walk forward, down the ramp of the box. She stood looking at the row of faces peering at her. Her ears, which had been pressed almost flat against her mane, slowly began to turn upright. We led her into her box which must have been heaven for Suey. She looked around and then to our joy walked across to the hay and having given it a few nudges with her nose began to munch. Our vet could find nothing wrong and neither could we. From the moment she arrived Suey became a fit donkey. My theory is that she had just had enough work and decided she was going to lie down until things got either better or worse! And people say donkeys have no intelligence!

Whilst life working outside with the donkeys was physically hard and had moments of sadness, it was extremely rewarding. It needed a lot of administration too.

Another member of office staff was necessary at this time and we took a girl qualified to do the accounts side of the work. Printing the leaflets to send one out with every reply became a chore, so our own small printing machine was installed, which I felt sure would save long-term costs. The machine cost nearly £2,000 and I had to take a very deep breath before ordering it. But it has proved worth its weight in gold now that we have a mailing list of donors who have contributed to the costs of the sanctuary during the last two years. Jan, the new girl, took to the printing machine like a duck to water and was soon able to make all her own plates.

Arranging advertisements was a difficult and important part of

our job, and Ken Birks, our advertising agent, and I spent hours working out the best approach to raise the necessary funds. Careful statistics of advertising effectiveness were kept to ensure we got at least a two hundred per cent return. The *Telegraph* or *The Times* brought in a very poor direct response but a lot of inquiries regarding covenants and legacies. As you probably know, covenanted income is very helpful to charities. Simply, it means that an individual taxpayer signs a form promising to pay us a fixed sum each year for four years.* We can then reclaim from the taxman the individual's basic-rate income tax on that sum. At present, this adds an extra three pounds to every seven pounds paid by the individual.

Legacies were something new to us, but having looked carefully through accounts of other registered charities it appeared that fifty per cent of their income was coming from them; so at this stage I invested a fair amount of advertising money by placing adverts in the type of paper that would attract legacies.

June Evers, who had been a great friend since the age of five, had recently lost her mother and was living alone in Exeter. As a result of a desperate plea from me she moved into one of our flats and became a trustee of the sanctuary. Trustee meetings were getting more frequent and it was absolutely wonderful having such a staunch friend living on site. As she was Superintendent of Radiography at the Devon and Exeter Hospital, her experience was also of great value. She replaced Judith Forbes, who had resigned as a trustee, being too involved with work on her own countryside parks.

We were trying to get as many donkeys as possible out into good homes and needed to build up a very careful form of inspection to ensure that we selected the right homes, and that the donkeys were visited regularly once they were out. Mr and Mrs Judge, who lived at the Farway Countryside Park, had been helping groom the donkeys regularly and they joined as our first two inspectors. Walther Brabæck, one of Niels' half-brothers, helped for a while, then Sheila Bazill took over. I designed special forms for them to take on their first visit which would

*This was changed in the 1980 budget to four years from seven years.

make sure they asked the right questions; once these had been filled in and sent back to us we studied them very carefully in the office to make sure the home looked right. In the past some of the mares had got into foal and we decided on a policy of only allowing geldings to go out, and only in twos. The inspectors now make three-monthly visits to see that the donkeys are in good health and that the farrier comes regularly.

Some of the people who sent us money were like Jean Bennett, an elderly lady who lived in Nottingham and who posted us a share of her pension every time she drew it. We named a donkey Jean after her and when Jean surprisingly gave birth to a little foal, Sunny Jim, we had great pleasure in sending a telegram to Mrs Bennett to tell her that her donkey had become a mother.

Other elderly pensioners from all over the country would write to us weekly, sometimes sending us as little as a 10p postal order each time. To these people our personal letter of thanks became a very real contribution to their lonely lives and they would write longer and longer letters. I found myself taking a personal interest in their welfare. Many people wrote to us from hospitals, and children galore saved their pocket money and sent it to us.

One regular donor was Jess, and she worked for a large insurance company in London. Her letter came regularly with the contributions from her fellow workers which she collected every week. A shock telephone call one day from a member of the staff brought the awful news that Jess had been killed in the Moorgate Tube disaster on her way to work and we were all heartbroken. Coincidentally, the morning that Jess was killed, My Poppett had given birth to her long-awaited foal, and so in memory of Jess's marvellous work for our donkeys the little foal was named after her. The company is still providing for Jess's upkeep and we receive a cheque for £150 a year.

Then there is a never-ending stream of letters regarding cruelty to donkeys in various parts of the country. These range from complaints about beach donkeys to conditions at markets and at donkey derbies, where donkeys are used to raise funds for other charities. The problem of beach donkeys has always been with us and some extremely good work has been done by the

108

Riding Establishments Act Committee who are affiliated to the British Horse Society. This committee was formed in 1968 to investigate conditions in riding establishments, to prevent the exploitation of horses, ponies and donkeys and to make sure that the legislation of 1964 and 1970 is complied with. They work in very close cooperation with the environmental health departments of local authorities and with veterinary surgeons in arranging licensing for each particular area. When bad cases on the beaches are reported to us, generally we liaise back through the REAC, as they are able to have the licence of the operator stopped if the complaints are found to be correct.

Conditions in the markets have never been good and led to the Ministry drawing up a new set of conditions about markets and donkeys which have now become law. The Donkey Sanctuary was asked for advice on this, and was pleased to be able to help.

Donkey derbies are another nightmare. Rules and regulations have been drawn up, one of which is that no rider will be permitted to ride if over eight stone. No driver or rider is allowed to carry whips, spurs or any other means of inducement for increasing the speed of the donkey. Whilst in theory this is fine, in practice the most enormous children and adults seem to ride the donkeys and complaints are received often accompanied by a picture from a local newspaper showing well-known personalities, rarely under eight stone in weight, galloping to the finishing line on a pathetic donkey literally bending at the knees.

Every complaint received in the office has to be investigated. Our only interest is in the welfare of the donkey and many of our letters as a result of the complaints receive extremely objectionable replies. Unfortunately Round Tables and other charitable organizations are often responsible for promoting donkey derbies and they never take kindly to being criticized about mistreatment. There is little we can do legally about such events other than complain to the local authorities, by which time, of course, it is far too late for the poor old donkeys.

Other letters relate to donkey racing, which is similar to donkey derbies. The Donkey Breed Society accept some racing run under the best possible conditions where the donkey rider is a child and the donkey is not made to look a laughing stock. But sometimes stallions are used and they can be dangerous and difficult for young riders to handle.

Our liaison with other animal charities on similar work has been reasonably good. Our funniest encounter was with the RSPCA inspector at Plymouth. He rang up one Friday night very late to say, 'Mrs Svendsen, what on earth can I do with two donkeys wandering in the centre of Plymouth?'

Nobody seemed to know where the donkeys had come from nor where they were going. We set off at the crack of dawn on the Saturday and picked up the two little donkeys, whom we called Plym and Duff, and put them into an isolation box. By Sunday morning we received a very irate call from their owner who had apparently gone away for the weekend and returned to find his pet donkeys escaped and sent to what to him obviously sounded a fate worse than death in a sanctuary! Plym and Duff were dispatched back to Plymouth on Monday and were the shortest-staying guests we ever had.

Bob Danvers Walker did a BBC radio programme called *The Countryside in Summer* and I did a talk with him from which we received an extremely good response, not only some very nice letters but also some large donations. Broadcasting always strikes me as nerve-racking until the first two minutes of the programme are over but the rewards for the donkeys make it so valuable. In organizing the sanctuary and administering its many sides we realize that every penny that we receive comes in from members of the public. I feel that our sanctuary doors should be open at all reasonable times for people to wander round and see for themselves what happens. Every single day the sanctuary opens from nine to five. We restrict it to these hours because people tend to leave gates open; once the evening round is done I like to feel that all the animals are secure and there is no danger of them being fed any food which could be harmful. We have never made a charge for people coming round the sanctuary, and perhaps because of this people have always been extremely generous. Our collection boxes are always well patronized and a genuine interest from the general public is a constant encouragement. A large number of children enjoy coming round the sanctuary, and we have one donkey in particular that always gets himself into trouble.

He's called Eeyore. He was the foal of Smartie, that poor little grey donkey that Niels and I carried down to our shed so many months ago. Eeyore was born surprisingly healthy and has been what can only be described as a cheeky little chap since his very first moments in life. If anything goes wrong in the sanctuary you can always gamble that Eeyore is involved somewhere. Hardly any gate or stable door is 'Eeyore proof' and if any of the old geriatrics happens to stand anywhere near the pond, Eeyore's favourite game is always to give them a slight nudge and push them in. In view of all the children's interest and with a view to raising further funds, I decided to write a children's book and chose Eeyore as my subject. Although the book was basically about how naughty Eeyore was, it gave the opportunity to tell children about the care of donkeys, how their feet were done and how they needed to be fed properly, in the hope that the message would sink home and the next generation would treat donkeys a little better.

The gentleman who had installed our printing machine had brought along a friend with him called Eve Bygrave who loved drawing and painting and wanted to try her artistic skill on donkeys. When I had written my book I suggested she might like to do some pictures to illustrate it with. This was the start of our partnership. I published it myself so that the Donkey Sanctuary could get the maximum money from the book. It was great fun being an unprofessional publisher, and with the Sidmouth Printing Company as my guide I became involved in different typesettings and type faces, paste-ups and all the other processes necessary to producing a book. Although *Eeyore, the Naughtiest Donkey in the Sanctuary*, looked at by the eyes of a professional publisher, is extremely amateur, it certainly began to sell in large numbers. From each book we sold for one pound, the Donkey Sanctuary got 78p, because doing the publishing myself cut the total expenses of producing the book to 22p.

During this time, I made a lot of visits to my parents who lived in Ottery St Mary, as neither was at all well. My father, who had never been strong, was ageing rapidly and becoming rather frail. When they wanted a holiday they would nip down to a hotel in Sidmouth so as to be near at hand; and thank goodness they did, because on 13 March I was rung from the hotel in the middle of the night to say that my father had had a stroke. Six days later he passed away quietly and my mother moved in to live with us.

Pat, my sister, had been married for many years by now, and her two sons, Michael and Peter, were grown up. She too was facing tremendous sadness at this time as her husband Derek was suffering from cancer. It was a very difficult time for all the family; the children found it hard to adjust to having their grandmother in the house, and the downstairs television room had to be turned into a bedsitter as she found the stairs a problem. We were extremely fortunate in that she was an easy person to live with, always gentle and kind to everybody. Her apple pies were legion and she loved nothing better than toddling off to make a cup of coffee and bring it through to me in the evening while I was still working in the office.

She played innumerable games of dominoes and cards with the children and in fact restored our family life to something like normal. She longed to have somebody to talk to. Weekend sailing with Niels had now become a thing of the past but I longed for his return on Sunday evening with his hilarious stories of the events at sea which cheered me into another world far away from donkeys.

By July 1976 the sanctuary had received £138,500 in cash, out of which we had been able to pay the purchase of Slade House Farm in full and also to purchase a further eight acres of field adjoining the sanctuary's fields. We had been able to buy a much-needed tractor, strengthen the floor of the barn to give room for another forty-five donkeys, and convert and equip the offices. The fencing had also taken a sizeable amount from our funds.

None of us felt it necessary to apply for a change of use for this eight acres, as we would only be grazing the donkeys on it. The planning people, however, thought differently. The first thing that made us aware of the brewing problem was a television feature from which I heard that a long council meeting had been held regarding the use of this land by the donkeys. But the television programme was so obviously sympathetic to the sanctuary that public opinion swung to our side and we never heard any more about having to get permission for an agricultural change of use.

I had to laugh one morning. There was a letter from a publican who wanted his donkey to come into the sanctuary as the field at the back of the pub had been taken over by the council for road widening. It wasn't the fact that the donkey had to come in that made me laugh but his request that the donkey should be given a pint of beer each day as it had developed a tremendous liking for it and wandered into the pub regularly for its pint. The staff were convinced I was having them on, but after the donkey arrived its frequent braying told us that something wasn't quite right. We tried him with his pint of beer and, my goodness, what a change, he became gentle and placid and everybody could handle him. However, within twenty-four hours he was ranting round his stable again and impossible to cope with. Once again a pint of beer produced a gentle placid donkey and we realized that we had our first genuine alcoholic on our hands!

It took us three months to wean the boozer from his beer by gradually giving him less and less each day and then adding water to make it weaker. But we managed; since then we have had two more alcoholic donkeys, including one called Bracken who could drink a whole pint without taking his lips off the pint mug, and no matter where he was in the field would gallop across at the clink of a pint mug.

Two more staff were needed during 1976. One person was now totally responsible for doing all the receipts and making up the orders for the *Eeyore* books. Eve Bygrave had produced some beautiful drawings which we turned into notelets and these we also sold. By Christmas she had designed a nice card which we printed ourselves, and that sold literally thousands in its very first year.

Health and Safety at Work rules had to be adhered to, a fire alarm system put in, and insurance requirements met because of the ever-present risk of a visitor being injured by one of our donkeys. We have only had one donkey that was very difficult. He was a six-year-old called Poly. His owner had telephoned us to tell us that the donkey was behaving in a rather aggressive manner and that she no longer felt she could keep him. We took him into the sanctuary and the result of a blood test showed that Poly was a rig. This is a technical term for a donkey who has been castrated, but where the castration has not been completely successful and one testicle has been retained. This often leads to a difficult-tempered animal and we certainly had a problem with Poly. The first time out of isolation we put him in a large field of geldings and he made such savage attacks on them all that we had to bring him back and put him in his own private box. We used to exercise him separately in the yard and introduced him to a friend with whom he eventually settled. However, very sadly one day whilst he was exercising in the main yard some visitors with a small girl walked through and with no provocation at all Poly bit the poor little girl on her arm, quite badly. Poly had to be put down as there was nothing we could do to ensure he was safe.

The weekly cost of looking after the 345 donkeys we had in care then was £783, and a further £292 per week was going on wages. The meteoric rise in the number of animals and consequent administrative work now required my full time and attention. It was decided that I should become the paid administrator of the sanctuary and in consequence Niels and I retired as trustees. Two new trustees were adopted – one was my sister, Pat Feather, and the other was John Morgan, who had been our bank manager for many years and was well regarded in financial circles. John Lovell joined the team as clerk to the trustees, and on this basis we looked forward to future years of expansion.

9 Work abroad and the Greek tragedy

The decision to help donkeys in other parts of the world resulted from the letters received concerning the appalling conditions abroad, which I couldn't ignore.

A new charity had to be formed, which was the International Donkey Protection Trust (IDPT), and as Rosalind de Wesselow was interested in the work we asked her to be one of the trustees. I also approached Colonel Norman Dodd, whom I had met previously in 'donkey circles' and who is a well-known journalist in the equine world. He and his wife Eileen are charming people and travel regularly to various parts of the globe. He agreed to help us and become a trustee. June Evers, Niels and myself made up the five trustees we felt were needed.

People had been sending small amounts of money designated to be spent on donkeys abroad, and by the time we called the first meeting on 27 January 1976 we had funds of £250 in hand and our application to become a registered charity had been accepted.

The documents signed, we decided to make an initial survey of countries to include South America, Ireland, the Middle East, Greece, North Africa, North America, Europe, Jamaica and Turkey. Wherever possible, two trustees would travel, and once a survey had been completed areas of work could be decided upon. Obviously the scope of our work would have to be limited by the funds available and I didn't really feel we could advertise a great deal until the initial survey had been done.

Some of the countries were out of reach as just the expense of getting there would have taken all our accumulated funds. However, Niels and his crew were sailing across to Cork in Southern Ireland on a big yacht race and I had already arranged to go over to be with him. This meant that whilst there, at no cost to the charity, I would be able to have a look around and see the conditions for myself.

It turned out to be quite an exciting trip. Two of the other crew's wives came with me, and there were two clear days before the men arrived after their somewhat arduous sail. Pam Jermyn, a well-known member of the Donkey Breed Society working in Southern Ireland, had a beautiful donkey stud and was keenly concerned about the welfare of Irish donkeys. She gave me an introduction to the Irish Society for the Prevention of Cruelty to Animals and a great deal of information on the problems in that part of the world. The state of donkeys' feet working in the peat bogs was bad, as was the general treatment meted out to the donkeys, many of whom were used for pulling small milk carts. There was insufficient work for our trust to spend a lot of money in Southern Ireland, I felt, and we could probably leave it to the Donkey Breed Society already working there and to the ISPCA to put their own house in order.

The men arrived the following day and we had two fabulous days before they set off on the return journey to Plymouth. Our flight home proved quite hilarious. I was wearing an emerald green suit and with Margaret Brook chose the front seat of the very small aeroplane that was flying us back to Plymouth. I remember there were also four nuns on the flight. The plane seemed to sit on the tarmac for a long time and we could see the pilot in the cockpit just in front of us looking round impatiently.

The stewardess walked past and I leant over and asked, 'What's the matter? Have we got some problems?' She replied, 'Yes, the co-pilot hasn't turned up.' 'I'll do it,' said I jokingly, laughing at Margaret, and to our immense surprise and horror the pilot beckoned me forward.

I just couldn't believe it was happening, but he said, 'Sit down and put the headphones on,' and so there I sat with the headphones on wondering what on earth to do next. He thrust a board on to my lap with a long check list on it and said tersely, 'Read those off.' I read out the strange names one after the other while he checked them off in the cockpit; then with a sharp 'Right, make sure your belt's fastened,' we were taxiing down the runway. Through my earphones I could hear the familiar call-up sign for St Mawgan, and as I felt I must add some contribution I mentioned it to the pilot. He nodded happily and then we had taken off and we were climbing up over Cork Airport. Once the course had been set he leant back in his seat and, through the little microphone he spoke into, asked, 'How long have you been a stewardess for Aer Lingus?' I realized then why I was sitting in the co-pilot's seat and didn't quite know how I should break the news to him. 'Um, I'm sorry, I'm not employed by Aer Lingus,' I said. His expression of dismay nearly sent me into hysterical giggles as he realized the mistake that he had made.

He was, however, extremely kind and when I explained I did have a wireless operator's licence and held my navigation qualifications he was a little happier. I sat in the co-pilot's seat all the way back to Plymouth and as we taxied up to the terminal I was quite disappointed Niels wasn't there to see me coming in.

I had been writing to all the countries suggested at the trustees' meeting and found a tremendous opposition from agricultural and veterinary officials to any suggestion that we should come over from England to help. But the situation was slightly different in Greece and Turkey.

We had taken on a housekeeper, Vanadia Sandon-Humphries, whom we called Noddy, to cope with the day-to-day running of the house. Noddy absolutely adored the donkeys as well as being particularly interested in the association of donkeys and handicapped children, and she helped outside when there was time and the opportunity. Her daughter's fiancé was Greek and his mother ran a very popular television chat programme which appeared regularly in Greece. Through Noddy I was able to arrange to present a programme about donkeys in Greece after being there for a week, and to show how the donkeys could be helped.

We also had a visitor at the sanctuary one Sunday morning whose name was Bora Paran. He was Turkish and was a reporter on a popular daily newspaper there. He was fascinated by the work we were doing in England, and when I explained about the charity formed to help people with donkey problems in other countries, he told me of the thousands of donkeys in Turkey which were an essential part of the economy and were in desperate need of help. We received a full page in the Turkish newspaper *Yenni Ashir* which included beautiful photographs in colour of the donkeys in our sanctuary and the work we were doing. Bora Paran offered to help me if I went to Turkey, and to provide us with a free translator and transport as long as the newspaper would be allowed to take pictures of me working. I contacted the World Federation for the Protection of Animals, who had representatives in Greece and Turkey, and they seemed more than willing for me to come.

For a long time Niels had been getting more and more worried at the amount of work I was doing and he persuaded me to take what was to be a dream holiday. With Alfred and Gloria Carpenter, Norman and Margaret Brook, and Peter and Rosy Calkin, our great friends, we decided to charter a yacht and sail round the Greek islands. After the holiday I would stay on in Greece and do the work there and then move on to Turkey and return home.

Once again flight costs could be shared and it was agreed with the trustees that I would pay half as I was going to have a holiday as well, and IDPT would only be responsible for me the day I started work in Athens. It seemed the most wonderful opportunity and I don't think I have ever felt I needed a holiday more.

After a good deal of poring over details we had booked a sixty-foot yacht named *Rusalka* and it was with great excitement that we arrived in Athens and walked along the quay to see our boat for the first time. The crew of the *Rusalka* consisted of Chuck and

Em Guest who, purely by chance, happened to live in Sidmouth, and a deck-hand called Claire. For the first three or four days I found it very difficult to unwind. My mind was still so much on the donkeys and the problems I had left behind that I found myself looking anxiously for donkeys as we came into each small harbour on the holiday. Those that we did see on the islands were extremely well looked after, and although they were carrying loads which seemed very heavy, the locals were being kind to them and there was no real need for concern.

It was on the island of Paros that my first problems arose. We went ashore for a quick drink and saw three mules waiting to take a load up to the village three miles away. Niels got into conversation with a man who was loading the mules and in error said that I was a donkey doctor. He immediately dropped everything and pulled me by the hand to look at the second mule, who was lame. I thought it was quite probable the mule had something in its hoof and Chuck who was with us went back to the boat to get my medical bag. I had taken the precaution before leaving England of making up a bag, with the vet's help, of what I thought I might need as a sort of first aid for donkeys. It contained a special ointment called Dermobian which was a great healer, an aerosol spray of terymycin for wounds and infections, acrimide powder which could be puffed on, a hoof-pick, and a surgical kit with local anaesthetic in case I came across any severe cases and had to stitch an animal up.

Chuck brought the case back and I got out my hoof-pick. It was the first time I had ever had dealings with the back legs of a mule and the first thing I noticed was the alacrity with which the owner went and held the head. After six unsuccessful attempts to pick out the hoof which kept flashing past my right ear, I gave up. The job was completely impossible. By this time it appeared that almost all the inhabitants of Paros had arrived and were standing around us in a large wide circle. Niels and the crew from *Rusalka* were looking equally concerned and it was going to be very difficult to retrieve what had now become a matter of national pride. I tried to look unconcerned and asked Chuck to pass me the terymycin can. There was a deadly silence as I held the can approximately a foot away from the mule's hind foot. There was quite obviously a swelling there and it appeared very likely that it had an infection of the fetlock. Aiming at the main swelling, I pressed the spray and a jet of purple terymycin hit exactly the right place. By the time the mule realized that medication had been administered and kicked out again it was too late. The treatment had been given. You could almost feel the air of relief amongst the crew and the awe of the crowd. The owner rushed up to me and thanked me most sincerely and after our drink we got back on the boat feeling pleased with the success of my first donkey mission.

We stayed the night in the bay off Paros, and the following morning I was treated with great respect wherever I went and was able to look at a lot of mules and donkeys on the island. None seemed over the age of about twelve years old and all seemed in reasonably good condition. The value of a mule on Paros appeared to be approximately £500, so no wonder they took such great care of them.

The next day we sailed to Santorini, a volcanic island. We anchored at the foot of the steep cliff on the top of which lies the village. The only way from the quay up to the village is by an almost vertical winding track, and a large number of mules and donkeys were standing at the bottom with saddles on ready to transport visitors up and down. At the time of our arrival ours was the only boat there and I wandered off to have a good look at the condition of the animals. There were a number of caves around and we went into some of these and found adequate supplies of alfalfa grass which had been dried for the mules to eat. I tried to persuade one of the owners to take a saddle off a mule but this he was reluctant to do and we soon discovered why. On our way up to the village we saw a large liner arriving which anchored just off the quay and within twenty minutes some two or three hundred tourists were clattering past us on the mules on their journey to the top. I was surprised to see that the mules seemed to enjoy the gallop up the long hill and even those without a rider would canter up alongside those giving rides. Once they got to the top the drover just gave one shout and the whole lot turned round and thundered back down to the bottom again.

We loved the village of Santorini and spent almost the whole day going round the little shops. For the first time on the holiday I felt really relaxed and well. It was a beautiful hot day and we were all beginning to get very sunburnt and fit. Early in the evening we took our little boat and went across to see the volcano which lies just off Santorini. You can anchor your boat at the bottom of the volcano and climb right up on to the rim and into the crater itself. The smell of sulphur was almost overwhelming and it was quite frightening at times to feel the bottom of one's shoes getting extremely hot. I was very glad to return to *Rusalka*.

Em and Chuck had invited us for a drink at the tiny taverna which was situated on the quay and it was almost pitch dark as we left *Rusalka* and found our way down the gangplank. There were one or two lights on the quay and taverna and as we made our way across we heard a strange clinking noise. One of the small donkeys that had been going up and down the quay all day was wandering around with a large chain round its neck. We could see it had some sores on its back and I told the others to have a drink whilst I just slipped back and got my medical bag to treat it. The bag was in my cabin and my mind was on nothing but the donkey as I made my way back to it. The aft hatch over the aft set of berths had been opened up wide for ventilation and in the dark the black space appeared as a hatch cover; in my haste I walked straight into it. I remember trying to grab hold of the hatch as I fell twelve feet to the deck below, but I was unable to hold on. Violent pain seared through my body and I lay partially winded and in such agony I was unable even to call out.

Em was busy cooking the dinner and heard the thud of my fall. I heard her come forward saying, 'Has somebody dropped something? Is something the matter?' And then she saw me. It was a great relief to know somebody knew I was there but I was unable to say anything to her at all as her anxious face came close to mine, and I heard her saying, 'My God, Betty, are you all right?'

She vanished for a moment and then reappeared with a blanket which she put over me and then I heard her going up on to the deck and running down the gangplank towards the taverna. I believe it was only a few moments before Niels was kneeling by me but it felt much longer. I found I was able to speak again and gingerly began to move each limb in turn to see what I had done. My left leg wouldn't move at all but my right leg seemed all right as did my left arm, but when Niels tried to lift me to move me on to a bunk the most excruciating pains shot through the upper half of my body and my left leg. I tried not to make too much noise as he put me into a more comfortable position and then sat by me holding my hand, tears slowly dropping down his face.

'Darling, what have you done?' he asked. 'Just when you were beginning to have a holiday. Why has this had to happen?' And then Chuck's anxious face was leaning over Niels. 'I will go and get a doctor,' he said. 'There must be a doctor somewhere in the village.'

Poor Chuck, he had to run all that way up to the town and eventually returned with the village doctor. Fortunately he spoke some English and without moving me he examined my leg and chest. 'I don't think she has done much damage,' he said, 'but I really think perhaps you ought to take her to hospital and have some x-rays. It is just possible she has broken something.'

Everybody looked round in dismay. Where was the nearest hospital? 'The nearest island with medical facilities is Siros, which is ninety miles away,' he continued. 'They have a municipal hospital and there is usually one doctor on duty. I suggest you set off as soon as you can and I will give her an injection which will take the pain away during the journey.'

He gave me an injection and left the boat. I could hear everyone in the dining room discussing what was to be done next and within ten minutes we were under way. It was decided not to use the sails as this would put the boat at an angle which would be difficult for me, and so with the engines at full steam ahead we set off for Siros. It was an absolutely nightmare journey. The injection he had given me seemed to do nothing at all and I could neither move nor breathe without extreme pain. My left leg was beginning to swell at an alarming rate and I now found enormous bruising appearing down the inside of my right arm. All through the night our friends kept popping in to see how I was doing, and Niels never left my side.

Eventually Niels said, 'Only a few minutes, darling, and we will be in.' And in the dawn we arrived at Siros. Chuck organized things very quickly and within an hour Niels came down to tell me that the ambulance had arrived to take me, and then the real problem started: how to get me off the boat. The doors were not wide enough for a stretcher to be carried through and in the end it was found the only way to get me out was the same way as I had fallen in – through the hatch. Once again they were unable to do this on a stretcher and I had to be lifted by my arms and pulled up through the hold by the ambulance men. I was almost unconscious as I was put on the stretcher and carried into the ambulance.

We arrived at the hospital and I still have no idea of what it looked like as I never saw more than the ceilings. I was wheeled into a large corridor where there were a large number of peasants milling around. They were all fascinated by my condition and my trolley was constantly pushed and knocked as people tried to get a better position to see what had happened. Eventually the doctor arrived and having a quick look he started shouting in rapid Greek. After that events moved very fast. I was wheeled into an x-ray room which reminded me of the very first pictures of x-ray equipment ever developed in the world! The machines were high and old fashioned and each time they were going to take a picture the men pushed a button and then ran for a little door which they slammed as they went through and then immediately reappeared through another door. If I hadn't been in such terrible pain I would really have found it rather funny, but under the circumstances I didn't feel like laughing.

After the x-rays, I was pushed back into the corridor and a heated discussion in Greek took place. I think one of the worst parts of an accident abroad is not being able to understand what people are saying, and the doctor seemed to be getting more and more anxious as he held up the five x-rays which had been taken. He showed these to everybody who wanted to look, including the crowd of locals which had now grown to quite enormous size.

'Please,' said Niels loudly. 'Can somebody tell me what's the matter? Can my wife go back or has she to stay in?'

One of the nurses spoke a little English. She put her hand on Niels' arm. 'Your wife will stay a long time,' she said slowly.

'She has broken five of her ribs and it is possible the liver is ruptured. A piece of rib has broken away and could make it worse. It is very dangerous. The doctor says if your wife moves she dies. Please tell her.'

With sinking heart I had heard the conversation and the doctor was now speaking rapidly to the nurse who was able to translate for us. I was wheeled through a very large ward and thankfully into a small private room at the end. Being lifted into bed was agony and I was terrified to move in view of the diagnosis. A nurse appeared with a large rubber bag and this was put over my liver. It was full of ice and extremely uncomfortable. Nobody made any attempt to put any strapping around the broken bones or even bothered to look at my left leg, which seemed equally painful to me.

Another nurse arrived with a large metal tray and the most enormous syringe I have seen for many years. It was the old metal type with a huge steel needle. What injections they gave me I still don't know but I got them every four hours and eventually my backside resembled the map I had made many years earlier to show where our Modeq dryers were distributed throughout the length and breadth of England.

They moved a camp bed in for Niels and, bless him, he stayed with me night and day. The crew sent a beautiful bunch of roses up and then regretfully had to set sail, as they were due to be back in Athens six days later for the end of the holiday. The next four days were indescribable. I was in constant pain day and night and nobody seemed to be able to do anything at all for me except to replace the ice bag every four hours. Eating was almost impossible as every time I even lifted my head the nurses told me the only English they had been taught for the occasion, 'You move, you die.'

They provided a straw and I drank a little greasy soup through it, but apart from that nothing else was possible. Niels got paler and paler and eventually he began to feel very sickly. We were convinced it was the terrible conditions. The hygiene of the hospital was almost zero; every morning the woman that cleaned the room with a filthy dirty mopping bucket would clean the communal toilet first; horrible brown smears would be left all over our floor when she went out. The needles that were used for injections appeared to have been used many times before they were re-sterilized, and if I happened to be the unlucky one to be treated after the municipal ward then it was a very painful injection indeed. By the fourth day we were both nearly ready to give up. Then fate stepped in once again.

Purely by chance a doctor from one of the big Athens hospitals who was on holiday called in at the hospital. He took one look at me and said to Niels, 'You must get your wife out of here immediately and into one of the hospitals in Athens. There is no doubt that if she doesn't have proper treatment she is going to die. If her liver does rupture here they have no facilities for operating and there is no way her life can be saved.'

We were both extremely frightened by his comments as we realized that they were probably very true. Niels rushed out to try to see the doctor but he refused to see Niels and the nurse who spoke a little English said, 'He is not happy that the other doctor has seen your wife and he says she must not be moved or else she will die.' Niels came back to me and said, 'Who can we contact in Athens, do you know anybody who might help?' I suddenly thought of Elli Evangelodou, the lady who was going to do the television interview with me in Greece. I had her telephone number amongst my papers and Niels rushed out to a phone box bearing this. I lay helplessly whilst he was away, concerned not only for myself but for Niels, who still seemed to feel constantly sick. He was back in an hour with a smile on his face for the first time.

'Darling, she was marvellous,' he said. 'She knows the Director of the Kat Hospital in Athens, which is apparently one of the best hospitals, and it has its own helicopter pad so if I can arrange a helicopter and get you there immediately she will have arranged it at that end.'

He rushed out again and within an hour was back. 'I have arranged for a helicopter tomorrow morning at ten thirty,' he said. 'It's going to cost £500 but we will just have to pay it. I've got to get you out of here.'

We spent a very bad night. I was used to being awake all night but Niels had eaten something that disagreed with him and he was uncomfortable with stomach ache for most of the time. The nurse who spoke a little English and had been giving us special attention slipped in and gave him some tablets which seemed to help the situation, but we were both grateful when the morning came and Niels could make arrangements to get me out.

The doctor was extremely annoyed we were leaving and tried to hold us up as I was carried out to the private ambulance Niels had hired. 'You will die,' were his last words to me as I left the hospital – not the most encouraging start to what was to be a very difficult journey to Athens! We were getting very concerned over time as the helicopter pilot had said he could only wait five minutes, having landed, and each minute over that would cost us an extra ten pounds. We arrived down at the quay and there was the helicopter waiting. Niels had brought a large blanket to carry me on, as the hospital was unwilling to lend us even a stretcher for the journey. They lifted me up in the blanket and hundreds of willing peasant hands managed to touch me on the short transfer between the ambulance and the front seat of the helicopter. One seat had been removed in the tiny aircraft so I could lie flat and Niels crouched beside me, his knees almost up to his chin with the suitcase propped on top as we took off and made the journey to Athens.

It was our first trip in a helicopter and I was very aware that it could easily be my last trip in anything. The pain was still intense and the doctor's words rang in my ears the whole time: 'You move, you die.' However, we landed safely and a luxurious ambulance pulled right by the helicopter to take me the 200 yards to the entrance of the hospital. I was put on a stretcher and once again wheeled along a long white corridor.

Niels completely vanished at this time and I began to panic slightly. I had moved a lot and I was still alive. I intended to stay that way, and tried to attract attention as best I could. 'Help,' I said hopelessly. 'I've lost my husband. Can somebody help me?' Eventually a very kindly-looking doctor bent down and asked, 'Are you English?' I was so relieved to find somebody speaking our language that I burst into tears and this seemed to do the trick, for within seconds I was wheeled into one of the consultants' rooms.

The last job my favourite nurse had done was to put another ice bag over my liver to last during the journey, and Dr Vranas, the specialist who was now looking after me, viewed it with horror as the blanket covers were removed. 'Whatever is this?' he asked. I explained that as my liver was punctured they had kept ice over the liver ever since the accident. 'How many days?' he asked tersely. 'It is five days now,' I replied. He grabbed the bag and threw it off. 'My God, you will be frozen. Your kidneys will have stopped working,' he mumbled. 'Why ever have they done this thing?'

'Sit up,' he said abruptly. I lay gazing up at him. 'But I can't,' I said. 'If I move, I die.' 'That was yesterday,' said Dr Vranas. 'You are here now. You don't die. Sit up.' And so for the first time in five days I was able to try moving my position. The joy of just being able to move without dying was overwhelming and despite the excruciating pain I managed to raise my shoulders off the pillows.

'Well done,' said Dr Vranas. 'OK. Now we start your treatment. You must go straight to x-ray and we will see how the ribs are getting on. Then we must look at this leg of yours and we will put you in a nice room and feed you up a little bit. I don't expect you have eaten much lately.' His kind face was almost too much for me and at that moment Niels came into the consulting room, having at long last traced me. He looked pale and drawn. 'Is she going to be all right?' he asked anxiously. 'Your wife will be fine,' said Dr Vranas. 'She just needs plenty of time to rest and recover, some good food and just a little bit of treatment.' He smiled at us both. 'She is a good friend of Elli Evangelodou and we will see she gets everything she needs.' He smiled and left the room.

The feeling of relief was indescribable. I wasn't going to die after all! We were taken through miles and miles of corridors and a large modern lift, and into the most super room overlooking Athens. It had its own private sitting room and bathroom; I was unable to get used to the luxury after the Siros hospital.

Above my bed was a special framework so that I could pull myself into a more upright position as it was impossible with my broken ribs for me to raise myself unaided. Once again they kindly placed a camp bed for Niels in the corner. Niels was not looking at all well.

'I wonder if I should tell the doctor about my stomach pains,' he said as we settled into our superb new room.

'Why don't you,' I said. 'He will be coming round to see me this evening.' And Niels agreed to do this.

At first Dr Vranas thought it was rather a joke Niels feeling ill as well but he did make him lie down and have a quick feel round his stomach. 'I think we will have another look at this again in the morning. Don't worry. Both get a good night's sleep and I am sure you will both soon feel better.'

Niels was able to make a call home to the children and the hotel that evening to tell them that at long last I was on the road to recovery and to give them our new telephone number. I was still on a drip as I was unable to eat properly, but for the first time I was given a small piece of goat's cheese for breakfast, which was a definite improvement on the revolting food on Siros. Niels was not feeling a bit well and when Dr Vranas came to see him at eight he sent him straight off down to have an x-ray. I was beginning to get extremely concerned. Niels never complained and had always been completely fit but he looked so grey and drawn and was feeling so sickly that it just couldn't be purely worry about me.

Within five minutes of Niels leaving the room, to my horror a large trolley was pushed in by two men wearing green gowns and masks. I was convinced they had come for me and was horrified that Niels wasn't there. Had my liver burst? I lay worrying myself silly but suddenly realized that the men were standing waiting for something and had no interest in me at all. Five minutes later the door opened and Niels was pushed in on a wheelchair. Without even letting him get off the wheelchair they bent forward, lifted him up, put him on the trolley and vanished from the room. You can imagine my feelings. I rang the bell frantically but nobody came and when eventually a nurse did arrive she couldn't speak any English!

'Dr Vranas,' I insisted firmly. 'Dr Vranas.' It was the only name I knew but she only smiled and shook her head and went out of the door. For two and a half hours I lay there waiting for somebody to tell me what was happening and getting more and more desperately anxious as Niels didn't return. Then suddenly the door burst open and four nurses came in wheeling a bed similar to my own. Without speaking they next pushed me nearer the window and put the second bed into place. All the bedclothes were stripped off it and a rubber sheet laid on with a single white sheet across it. There was no pillow. Drip stands were brought in and set up next to the bed, and I could only lie in horor trying to think what was happening.

A quarter of an hour later the door was pushed wide open again and in came a trolley. There were two nurses at either side of Niels, both holding drips high above him, and Niels was completely unconscious. The men lifted him on to the bed; the nurses fitted the drips to the two drip stands by the bed and then everybody left. I lay looking across at Niels, tears pouring down my face. Whatever had happened to him? My poor Niels. Fortunately at that moment Dr Vranas walked in. I hardly recognized him in his green operating gown but he came straight across and sat down on my bed taking the mask away from his face as he did so. He held my hand and said, 'I'm sorry, dear. You really do seem to have got problems between you. Your husband's appendix burst some time last night and by the time he was x-rayed he already had acute peritonitis. We have done our best but there is still some danger for the next few hours. Don't worry, we will do everything we can for you both.'

Niels' first words when he became conscious some hours later were typical: 'Did they really need to do it? I never get ill.' But alas this time he really had.

The following morning at six o'clock I looked across to Niels and saw his eyes were wide open. 'Do you know, darling,' he said seriously, 'before they would accept you into this hospital I had to guarantee £1,000 and pay every single drachma I had on me to the registrar, and now I am ill too. I do hope our insurance is going to cover all this.'

'I don't mind,' I said feelingly, 'as long as we get out of here alive.'

Niels, of course, has an extremely strong constitution, but I am pleased to say that I managed to get out of bed before he did! I had to ring England and tell them that it was now Niels on the danger list, not myself, and I could just imagine the concern my phone call must have aroused at home!

129

The hospital was absolutely wonderful. I had been lying thinking miserably in Siros, 'Why on earth did this happen to me when I was only trying to help animals?' It did all seem so unfair, but now the reason had been made clear. As Dr Vranas had said, had Niels not been in hospital when his appendix burst then he would have died. We found later that the *Rusalka* became storm-bound on her journey home to Athens. At the very time Niels' appendix burst she was sheltering from the gale in the lee of an uninhabited island almost 200 miles from the nearest port.

On the last day of our stay in hospital Elli Evangelodou came to see me with the secretary of the Hellenic Animal Welfare Society, Patricia Stethatos. They were so concerned to see our condition, which had caused considerable interest amongst all the staff and patients in the Kat Hospital. They promised me full cooperation and the chance of a broadcast the following year if I would come back to Greece, and this I promised to do.

Arrangements for the journey home proved very difficult. The hospital was very good and rang British Airways and they came to our bedside to arrange tickets and travel arrangements. It meant two stretchers, two wheelchairs, two special seats and similar arrangements to meet us at London Airport. Our bank at Ottery St Mary cabled out £1,500, which was our bill from the hospital, and almost six weeks after leaving England for our holiday of a lifetime we were both laid out in the first-class compartment of a British Airways plane. Never had we been so pleased to see British Airways in all our life and they treated us most royally. We were both given a free half-bottle of champagne and the pilot came to talk to us after take-off. Having seen the intense pain that the ascent had caused me he arranged with London Airport for a long approach to prevent any further discomfort for me.

Niels had a large Citroën estate car and Peter Feather, my nephew, who was managing the hotel, was waiting to meet us from the ambulance at London Airport. He had made the back of the car into a bed, and Niels and I lay together side by side on the long journey back to Devon. We did get one good laugh when Peter had to fill up with petrol and the startled petrol attendant suddenly became aware of Niels and me lying in the bed at the back. Seeing his startled expression, Peter explained quietly, 'Well, you see, they are on honeymoon. I am only the chauffeur. This is the way they wanted it.' And he got back into the car and drove off.

After this expedition I decided not to go on the return trip to Greece and Turkey on my own, and so June Evers, my friend and trustee, came with me the following year, in March 1977.

Pat Stethatos was kindness itself, and after a five-day tour of Greece I was able to see many of the cruelty problems for myself; these were indeed intense. On the mainland the attitude to the donkeys was very different to that of the peasants on the islands. We saw the most terrible sights including donkeys with their eyes poked out by sticks and the most savage beatings which even my medications could not ease.

We worked very hard whilst over there and the television programme proved a tremendous success. Through interpreters I was able to explain how much more the donkeys could help the peasants if they were treated better and I appealed for less weight to be put on the donkeys' backs.

Very few vets are concerned about the care of donkeys in other countries as the owner of a donkey generally cannot afford to pay for a vet. They seemed quite surprised that anybody would take particular interest in them, looking on them purely as a beast of burden. The situation in Turkey was slightly better whereas on the Greek islands the value of the animal to the economy was recognized; and whilst some were in desperate trouble it was only fair to say that the children of the peasants suffered equally. I think the donkeys got as much food as the rest of the family.

Our help here was so greatly appreciated that we realized the use of our charity. The peasants were desperate for medications, and once they learnt we had come into a village they would queue outside almost all night so that we could treat their animals in the morning before moving on. We spent nine days in Turkey and decided we must return there the following year.

Our next mission was to North Africa and the Middle East and we linked up here with two charities already working in these areas: the Society for the Protection of Animals in North Africa, which covers Tunisia, Libya and Algeria, and with Brooke Hospital in Cairo, which tackles Egypt. We met a tremendous number of donkeys and an equivalent number of donkey problems. Apart from treating donkeys and mules, SPANA look after dogs, cats and other animals and they seemed particularly interested that a charity should concentrate just on donkeys and mules.

Once again, on ageing all the animals I found very few aged over fourteen or fifteen and began to wonder if there was any specific reason for this. It was quite possible it was the overloading, although this certainly wasn't so in every case I saw as donkeys were doing many different jobs, such as turning water wheels, being used for driving carts, and for ploughing. I wondered if it could possibly be too many parasites in the gut, and answers to my many questions seemed to point to this factor.

Many donkeys seemed to die with severe pains in the stomach which the vets put down to colic. I began to think this could be a large dose of worms which eventually ruptured the gut. The cooperation from SPANA was magnificent and we arranged to visit them the following year to follow up our work and to help with their programme to exchange the cruel bits which are used on the donkeys. We had taken twenty-four bits over with us and these were used within our first two days' work.

We would start work at 6 a.m. when it was cool and by twelve o'clock in the morning we would sometimes have treated over 200 donkeys in the various souks. Conditions were extremely primitive and by the time we went on to Egypt neither of us was feeling particularly well. The Egyptian part of the tour proved similarly difficult. The Brooke Hospital proved a real oasis for animals in the middle of Cairo and the cases of deliberate cruelty we saw in this part of the world were heartbreaking. We found not only animals suffering this fate but also children who were still being sold into private households as servants at the age of five and contracted to these people until they married.

We went out with the Brooke Hospital and worked with them in the souks where our terymycin spray and Dermobian cream were in frequent use and relieved the suffering of many poor mules and donkeys. By the third day in Egypt we were both becoming very ill. The fleas which affected us did not come from the donkeys but from the many Arabs that pressed around us the whole time we were working. I would finish treating an ulcerated sore on a donkey's chest and find I was physically unable to stand up properly because of the Arabs all around me. They were often crawling with fleas and these would drop on our arms, hair and legs as we worked. We were staying in cheap hotels to save money for the charity and nine out of ten of these did not possess proper washing facilities. We frequently had only a tap and a bucket of cold water and this economy on the hotels proved very false. June's legs began to swell as the bites went septic and we both had some form of dysentery. What a relief it was to return to England three days before the tour was due to end.

I was raising funds for our work through appeals in the news-letter which I was now writing, and the following year we arranged to visit the isolated parts of Turkey we had previously visited where the donkeys were having such trouble. A cheap way of visiting was to use the boat *Small World* which carried twenty-four passengers and spent one or two days at many small ports along the west and south coasts. We decided to set up a worm-dosing programme and purchased collars for the donkeys we were going to treat; I was now convinced that the reason for the early death of the donkeys was the parasite infestation. We took a small laboratory which we set up in our cabin on *Small World* and which included a microscope through which we could examine the dung samples. The Turkish newspaper *Yenni Ashir* had already produced another double-page colour feature on the work to be done and had set out an itinerary of where we were going to land so that the peasants could bring their donkeys down to the quaysides. Despite our preparations and investigations before the trip started it proved an absolute disaster.

We landed at the small ports where the donkeys had been in profusion the year before to find no donkeys at all. We found the odd one and took dung samples from it and treated it with the anthelmintic we had carried to prevent worms, duly examining the samples back in the cabin. It was very difficult working with the microscope as either the boat was moving or, when in port, the generators were on, causing a certain amount of quiver and making analysis of the samples very difficult. However, we persevered and amongst the few animals we were able to test we found a tremendous incidence of both eggs and live larvae. By the time the boat had reached Antalya, its furthest port east, we were almost desperate with worry. We had only treated twenty-three donkeys and we knew we were wasting our hard-earned funds.

All along the coast in the boat we had kept noticing numerous polythene-sheeted greenhouses which had not been there the year before. Were these anything to do with our problem? In Antalya we went to the local agricultural office, where we met the veterinary surgeon for the area; he refused to believe that all the donkeys had vanished. He produced hundreds of figures which showed that there were donkeys everywhere and eventually we tied him down to one area called Kas approximately 200 kilometers along the coast and where we knew our boat would be calling at the end of its tour. We made our way with great difficulty overland. It was a 24-hour journey as it was frequently broken by long waits at the roadside for mountain roads which had subsided to be relevelled. We finally arrived, exhausted, in Kas, having carried all our laboratory equipment and our medical gear with us, and managed to find a very small boarding house where we had a clean bare room with two beds and a tap in the side of the wall with a bucket, which was to be our only washing facilities.

We both lay on our beds and I was almost dropping off to sleep when a terrible yell from June caused me to sit bolt upright.

'Help, Betty, look over your head,' she cried and there was the biggest spider I had ever seen; he must have been as big as my hand and was firmly ensconced in the corner. 'As long as that stays in this room I am not staying,' said June, and she vanished through the door.

I undid my belt and by standing on the bed and flicking the spider with the end was able to drive him to the wall over the open doorway, and eventually to my great relief he crawled under the lintel and out into the corridor. June returned in as dignified a manner as possible and once again we collapsed on our beds. It was to be a short-lived rest, however, and it could only have been ten minutes before the mosquitoes and flies began to make their presence felt. Gradually the room began to fill and all thought of rest driven from our minds as we desperately sprayed fly killer from my medical pack.

By evening the situation was untenable and with grim determination and June's full permission I searched the corridor until I found our unwelcome spider and gradually reintroduced it to our bedroom. We all lived happily together with no flies for the rest of our stay.

You can imagine our disappointment in Kas to find that instead of 1,870 donkeys promised by the agricultural officer there were exactly three. I don't think three donkeys have ever been more thoroughly examined and once again the dung samples tested were full of all types of parasites. We were pleased to see the boat call in on our last day. That morning June had narrowly missed putting her foot into her shoe in which a scorpion had been sleeping!

It really wasn't one of our best trips and it was good to be back in England. On our return, thinking of the many greenhouses and tomatoes being grown, I rang Heinz in London to see if they could be connected in any way. They told me they had been trying to help the economy of poor areas by encouraging the peasants to set up greenhouses for growing tomatoes and were deeply concerned that their help had in some way affected the welfare of the donkeys.

In June 1979 we returned to North Africa to work with SPANA, and it has proved our most successful trip. With the completed cooperation of SPANA we dosed over 1,000 donkeys in the area and we worked night and day in our laboratory examining samples and keeping very careful records of each donkey treated. In addition to the worming doses, we dealt with innumerable saddle sores and wounds and were able to help the valuable work done by SPANA in this area. We set up a proper research programme using twelve donkeys which had a complete medical examination, took samples which were fully analysed. SPANA will administer the treatment which we started every two months until we return to check the health of these particular twelve donkeys. We hope to prove that we can not only extend the donkey's life by anything up to ten years but that we can make it a much fitter and healthier life. A great deal of the suffering of these poor donkeys in all parts of the world is caused by their lack of nourishment and the small amount they do receive having to be shared by a myriad of parasites to which they are host.

Our most exciting trip has been to South America, in November 1979, the direct result of a bequest. I think the report published by Bob Forbes, our publicity officer and BBC freelance journalist, sums it up very well:

Mercy mission to South America

The donkeys of South America are in fine fettle. That is the general

conclusion reached by animal lover Betty Svendsen following a 15,000-mile fact-finding mission.

From oil-rich Venezuela, where petrol is 10p a gallon, to the arid wastes of Peru and the green Andean Valleys in Ecuador, she found that the South American values his working donkey.

Mrs Svendsen, who runs a donkey sanctuary at Salcombe Regis, near Sidmouth, headed a team of four – others were Mr Andrew Trawford, the sanctuary's vet, Miss June Evers, a trustee, and Mr Bob Forbes, journalist and broadcaster – who returned this weekend after a month-long trip.

The project was financed by a legacy left specifically for the expedition by a Miss Cook's Trust. Mrs Svendsen, who founded the International Donkey Protection Trust, says in her report:

'At the end of the tour to South America I feel a strange mixture of pride and humility. I am proud of the way the donkey helps humanity in this part of the world, a gentle, patient beast of burden, never complaining, often working almost completely alone carrying enormous loads from the fields to his owner's house. Pride in that his near-starving owner treats him with care and often affection and to the best of his ability, and humble in that people in such near or starving conditions can retain their pride, keep themselves so clean and be so dignified in their appalling state.

'I have been so lucky to have such a good team on this trip, which at best has been hard, at times almost disastrous. In our search for the truth regarding donkeys and their conditions in this vast continent, we have had to leave the main highways and tourist areas, and have literally taken to the hills. Maps have proved inaccurate and even the best navigations have found us on impassable roads in temperatures up to 100 degrees with hired cars which tended to break down at regular intervals. Add to this the attentions of strange biting insects, accommodation not always of acceptable standard and the sort of food we had to live on, and it is clear why teamwork has been vitally important to the overall success of the trip.

'We have seen over 1,000 donkeys since leaving the UK and with a few notable exceptions have treated every one in need. In Venezuela we found large herds of feral donkeys, living a completely natural existence. These we were unable to get near, but this country we found rich and advanced and the donkey almost extinct as a working animal. In Peru and Ecuador, however, the picture was extremely different and the donkey an important part of every village and hill community. The more inaccessible the village the more necessary the donkey.

'Our help was received with gratitude, once the people were assured our help was *libre* (free) and donkeys were brought to us from all parts of the village. We treated some ulcerous sores, many rope burns from tethering and almost all for parasites. Generally in Peru the donkeys, cattle, sheep and goats were kept in a communal compound, so our work was made easy, but in Ecuador in the villages where we worked, 10,000 feet up in the mountains, each little shack had its donkey in the yard. The owners were mainly Indians and their care of the donkeys good.

'Unlike our work in other parts of the world, there were no terrible mouth wounds. None of the donkeys wore bits in their mouths and they are proved here to be totally unnecessary. A tremendous amount of suffering to donkeys could be saved in other parts of the world by emulating their example.

'The fact that we found no old donkeys could be for two reasons, either, as in other parts of the world, they die due to parasites, or, as we were told to be fact in northern and southern Ecuador but were unable to confirm personally, they are slaughtered at the age of ten to twelve years to provide much-needed food for a starving population. In either event I feel the donkeys in this part of the world have a much more cared for life than their brothers in Africa and the Middle East.'

The films made in South America by June Evers, provided and developed by the BBC, got nationwide showing; the great interest of the public resulted in a financial gain for the charity.

The next trip for IDPT is to be an exploratory trip to Southern Spain by Rosalind de Wesselow and Pat Feather following up the many cases of reported cruelty. If on their week's tour they find the donkeys in real need their trip is to be followed by one encompassing a fully equipped medical team. June Evers and I are due to return to the North African deserts with our laboratory and a BBC film crew to follow up our past two years' work, and to examine the twelve donkeys treated with our anthelmintics every eight weeks since our last visit – the reports received from El Haj M. Abderrahman Lejri, the senior SPANA vet, are highly encouraging with a 'significant improvement in the condition of the twelve treated donkeys'. We are looking forward to seeing them. If this improvement is the case, then a very practical way to help the starving of the Third World would be for governments to provide free anthelmintics for donkeys and mules so that they can live healthier, longer lives to the general benefit of the starving peasants who rely on them.

Looking at Timothy, I couldn't believe that anybody could have done such a thing to a donkey. He had been sent to us by the Horse and Pony Protection Society, who had rescued him after both his ears had been almost severed right through by vandals wielding carving knives. They had found it very difficult to keep him happy there and they felt that as specialists we would probably deal with his problems better than anyone else. For almost two months we were nearly beaten. Timothy would allow us nowhere near him without attacking us both with his mouth and his front hooves, which he used to great effect. We had a big notice outside his isolation box warning staff not to go in singly as he could trap someone in a corner and do them serious injury.

We tried him with other geldings out in the yard to see if he would make a friend but Timothy attacked every donkey we let near him and nobody seemed to want him. In the next box were Henry and Henrietta, two devoted elderly donkeys who had been sent in together, Henry unfortunately with a severe heart complaint. One night I was doing my evening rounds and to my horror found Henry in the final throes of death following a heart

attack. Comforting him as best I could whilst I waited for the vet, I let Henrietta out into the corridor as I needed all the space I could for Henry, who died within five minutes of the vet's arrival. There was nothing anyone could have done to save him.

As the vet and I went into the corridor, to my surprise there was Henrietta with her head right over Timothy's box and they were gently nuzzling each other. I was almost unable to accept the sight before my eyes, it was so unusual for Timothy, and I quietly opened the door of his box and Henrietta went straight in. From that moment on Timothy changed. We were able to take the notice down from outside his stable and within another three months the attack with the forward hooves had become a gentle shake of the hoof. With Henrietta we were able to introduce him into the geriatric unit and with her care and constant companionship Timothy has now settled down and is enjoying his life at the sanctuary.

It was becoming quite apparent that our facilities at Slade House Farm were being overworked. The donkeys were still coming in at the rate of approximately six a week from all over the country; wherever a donkey got into trouble they seemed to be sent to us, and provided the request was genuine we turned no donkey away.

We began to look for another farm and found one on the market called Brookfield, near Honiton, which seemed ideal. This time there were 127 acres and extremely large outbuildings and barns which would be ideal for the donkeys. The farm went to public auction and the sanctuary was able to buy it at a very good price. We were horrified the following day to find criticism pouring in on us from all sides – in particular, from farmers who were worried that we were using up good agricultural land. Brookfield had not been run as a farm, in fact, and its previous owner had been using all the barns and the outyards for his engineering business, so we really couldn't see what all the fuss was about. Most of the farm was on very sloping ground and the only agricultural use it had had was that its previous owner had allowed the adjoining farmer to graze his sheep and cattle over it at certain intervals. Despite the criticisms we completed the purchase and Charles Courtney, now my secretary Julie's husband, who had been working on the farm for six months at Slade, moved into the bungalow with Julie and took over as manager there. Charles had trained at Seal Hayne College and had an extremely good eye for the donkeys. Within a very short time of his first group arriving he knew every single one by name and could explain in detail any problems any individual donkey was having to the vet on his regular visits.

John, of course, was in overall charge of both farms and arranged for the alterations at Brookfield. We had to buy another tractor as it was obviously impractical to move the one from Slade House Farm every time it was needed at Brookfield, which was five miles away; and we had to take on yet another employee to help Charles. By this time 374 donkeys had been received into the sanctuary and we placed 130 of these at Brookfield.

My sister's husband, Derek Feather, was at this time seriously ill in hospital. The cancer had extended from his leg, which had had to be amputated, to other parts of his body, and after a long-drawn-out and extremely painful period Derek died in June 1976. Pat was heartbroken and exhausted after the two years' struggle against ever-increasing odds. I hate funerals and always have had a problem with being deeply affected by death when it seems too soon. Derek had always been such a gentle, kind man; he had spent his whole life working hard and helping everybody, bringing up his family, and to be struck down just at the age when he should have been able to relax perhaps a little more and enjoy himself seemed very cruel. Working extremely hard, long days and evenings with no let-up in work and no weekend time off at all, together with this tragedy, made me get rather miserable and low.

Niels persuaded me to spend the weekend yachting with him, and we went in for our first cross-Channel race to Treguire on the coast of Britanny. Lise, Paul and Clive came with us as crew with Jeremy, out local doctor, and Guy Thornley. It was a fantastic experience to be away at sea and have nothing to think about except the thrill of the race. To our surprise we were first past the finishing post and had the most marvellous weekend gorging ourselves on delicious French food. Our sail home was reasonably uneventful despite a force-seven gale which blew up on the way and we got home safe and physically tired after a particularly needed break.

Niels was managing to sail every weekend but I found it harder and harder to get away. I now had fourteen employees to look after apart from the donkeys and the need for keeping our heads above water financially was absolutely essential. Having published the book about Eeyore and sold 744 copies in the first three weeks, I decided to try my hand at writing a newsletter for the many people who contributed to us. It had been suggested to me by the Charity Commission as a good way of keeping in contact with our many donors; so with some trepidation I wrote the first newsletter, which went out to 18,000 people. My carefully kept customer-record cards, typed on a special addressograph letter proved invaluable as we bought a machine which printed the labels *en bloc* and cut out the work to a great extent.

It was a very simple newsletter and told briefly how the charity had started and of our problems during the last six months. It ended up with an appeal for funds for both the Donkey Sanctuary, the International Donkey Protection Trust and the Slade Centre, all of which were now separate registered charities. The response was overwhelming. Almost everybody seemed to send us much-needed donations and our income soared. Visitors were arriving in increasing numbers and Julie and I devised a walk-round visitors' room in a disused outbuilding where they could see pictures of the donkeys as they came in and then go and visit the actual donkeys to see the improvement for themselves. Visitors saw notices in Niels' hotel and local press. This went down very well and again funds increased.

Encouraged by the success of *Eeyore* I wrote another book called *The Donkeys' Christmas Surprise*. It was a very simple story about four of our donkeys here and their wish to help Father Christmas pull his sleigh when the reindeer got ill. Many children write to Father Christmas c/o the GPO and, of course, they don't get a reply, and so on the back of the book we gave an invitation for the children to write to the donkeys to tell them what they would like for Christmas; and every child that wrote in got a reply and a picture of a donkey.

This time Eve Bygrave did beautiful oil paintings in colour and

142

we priced the book at £1.50. Although the sales were not so good as those of *Eeyore* they certainly helped our income.

Encouraged by the response of the children to these books and saddened by the many donkeys still arriving in terrible condition with overgrown hooves, malnutrition and other diseases caused by ignorance rather than direct cruelty, I wrote a lesson for schoolchildren which I hoped would prevent the next generation of donkeys being so badly treated. It took a great deal of time to write this as it obviously had to be factually accurate, but eventually I managed to finish it and it was sent out to 19,000 schools.

We had recently received a very bad load of donkeys that had been removed from a beach by the RSPCA and as a result of this I was reminded of Suey's arrival and wrote *The Story of Suey*. We sent a copy of this to the schools in coastal regions and in the back I drew the children's attention to the regulations concerning working donkeys on the beach in the hope that thousands of schoolchildren would help us in our job. This indeed has turned out to be the case and we receive numerous reports now from our young watchdogs around the coast.

We received so many replies from schoolchildren that a new member of our office staff had to be taken on just to deal with the correspondence from the schools. Gradually as the lesson became more widely circulated throughout each school we began to receive donations of very substantial sums as the whole school got together to raise funds either for the Donkey Sanctuary itself or for the handicapped children we were helping through our Slade Centre.

It certainly lightened many of my days when I would receive an enormous envelope with perhaps twenty-five letters written by the children of a particular class illustrated by their idea of what our donkeys looked like! This liaison with schools has gone one stage further now and many of them visit us on a regular basis.

Between September and December 1976 my work was greatly restricted by the Greek injuries but fortunately a lot of the written work could be done from my bed and with a telephone next to me I was able to keep in touch with things. Oh, I desperately missed being able to see my donkeys, and one of the worst things was having to lie in bed listening to the donkeys braying in the middle of the night and knowing I was unable to go out and see what was the matter.

I recovered sufficiently by 15 December to be able to come down and help the staff with the Christmas rush. A series of advertisements was appearing in the national press and the *Radio Times* and I had also written a second newsletter, which we sent out early in December. The result was absolutely shattering. I don't think our post office knew what had hit them as letters began coming in at the rate of six hundred a day, the excitement of a great sack of mail. On every advert after our appeal for funds we would say, 'Please write to the Donkey Sanctuary,' and if the advert was in the *Radio Times* it would be followed by a code such as 'RT4' if that was the fourth insertion in the *Radio Times*. The *Daily Express* would be 'DEx', *Sunday Telegraph* 'ST' and when it came to the *Sunday Express* we found ourselves writing 'SEX' over all the replies! As the letter was opened its contents were listed and its source was carefully put on to the records. Just opening the post when there were six hundred letters would take five and a half hours and then every donor had to be thanked and the money listed and banked.

Christmas that year was particularly beautiful at Salcombe Regis church. We had a very old set of handbells, and we arranged for somebody to come and teach us to use the bells, but after the first meeting our tutor was unable to attend again. So for light relief I wrote some easy bell-ringing music and with a very gallant team of bell-ringers we struggled to get our standard of perform- ance up to concert pitch for Easter morning. During the first few practices which we held in our house even my mother rang the bells, and these sessions usually ended in hysterical laughter as my mother always seemed to toll her big bell at the wrong moment. But soon we moved down to the church and became a little more professional. I was more nervous as I conducted the simple Easter piece I had written than I have ever been when making a broadcast or asked to lecture or speak! But I think everybody enjoyed it.

Encouraged by the start we had made, the church committee agreed to buy a new set of bells so that we would be slightly less handicapped at our next event. Regretfully once again, due to pressure of work, I had to pass over my job to another willing volunteer. I just hadn't any more time for bell-ringing.

On 29 December 1976 I did a broadcast for *Woman's Hour* and this brought a good response, not least from a large number of women's institutes and Rotary clubs asking me to give lectures at their various meetings. At first these lectures were very difficult, particularly as they came after a hard day's work in the sanctuary, but gradually I got more confident and found the enthusiasm of the audience helped me greatly. In some cases, particularly with Rotarians, I would be asked for lunch first and then to speak and the normal time allowed is twelve to fifteen minutes. To tell my story in this time was almost impossible and I had to develop a very cut-down version which would go down in the brief time allowed. I found that the businessmen were more interested in how I ran the business side than in actual details of donkeys, so I was able to slant the lecture in their direction. Women's institutes, however, wanted to know all the problems, like how did I manage at home with all the donkeys? And, in what sort of condition did the donkeys come in? The questions after the meeting were always pertinent, and donations were generously given. I found lectures to the deaf rather difficult as I am not good at speaking through a microphone, particularly when this is pitched very high for the hard of hearing.

The lecture I think I have enjoyed most was given to the Bath City Guild. Their members came to Sidmouth for a week's holiday and I went to their hotel. I really did receive the most tremendous reception there and almost the whole guild came back to visit the sanctuary a year later and it was just like meeting old friends.

By January 1977 I was still not well enough to go skiing and so we had to split up for our children's holiday that year. Niels went skiing with Clive; Paul was in the RAF, so June and I took Sarah on a three-day trip to London. Lise was still attending the Rachel McMillan Training College, where both Pat and I had been on a full-time teacher-training course, and she and her fiancé joined us for a lightning tour of London. It was lovely to relax with the children and we went to almost every gallery and museum in London. We took Sarah to see the *Sooty Show*, which was in the little theatre underneath the Savoy Hotel. The show had just nicely got under way when a party of four German adults arrived and pushed past us to their seats in the middle of the row. After watching the show for ten minutes the German turned to me and said, 'I thought this was a Smutty Show, what is this Sooty?' And I had to explain to him that he had got things slightly muddled up! It caused considerable amusement when with very red faces they left the theatre.

In the early spring Guy, our partner in *Bandolier*, with whom we had spent many happy hours sailing together in the waters off Plymouth, contracted cancer and died within three months, leaving us with no alternative but to sell the boat. It was a very sad time and I can never forget my sorrow when with his widow and Jeremy and Anne Bradshaw Smith we scattered his ashes from Salcombe lifeboat on the waters he had grown to love.

With the money from the sale Niels bought the hull of a thirty-four-foot yacht to fit out himself in our own garden. It certainly kept him busy and the family named the boat *Jaws*. Niels got an artist to paint a very realistic shark's mouth on the bow of the boat and night after night he would be in the boat hammering away to get it ready for Easter in three months.

Although I always had to do early-morning rounds and work when required on Sunday, I always tried to put aside some time for the family, and used to cook enormous Sunday lunches. Some single members of the staff were living on the sanctuary and they came in to make it a real family luncheon. Niels shared the purchase of the boat with his friends Norman and Eric, and most Sundays they would come along and help as well and so we would be a big party of between twelve and fourteen. Noddy, now working full time with the donkeys and handicapped children, agreed to do the Sunday lunches so I could go to church; I loved singing and had been offered a place in the Salcombe Regis church choir. I was able to continue singing in the choir for two years until the pressure of work at the sanctuary got so great that I very regretfully had to give it up. We were an extremely small choir of only seven, so every voice really counted. Generally I sang contralto but we lost our only tenor and the choir mistress

146

asked me to take on the role of the tenor. I don't think I ever quite fitted this properly!

Amongst the particularly sad donkeys that came in at that time was Angus. He was covered with small growths which turned out to be cancerous and one or two of these were very large and difficult. Our vets developed an extremely good technique for cryosurgery (a form of deep-freezing) and with no pain to Angus they were able to deep-freeze these and the worst of them were then removed surgically. The treatment became known as 'Angus cryosurgery' in the veterinary world, so I really feel that this old donkey, having been rescued, certainly did his part to help younger donkeys suffering from similar disease. We had previously treated several donkeys unsuccessfully but it certainly enabled Angus to enjoy his old age with us without being troubled by his painful growths.

I was getting a little concerned now at the number of staff we had to employ to keep up with the ever-increasing volume of work coming in. Our accountants worked out some figures for us as I was anxious to see that not too much of each pound sent in was spent in fact on administration. It was interesting to note that on their figures only 7.69p of every pound received went on to the administrative side, the rest going directly to the donkeys. I checked the figures of other charities and found very few as low as ours; it seemed that we were working along the right lines.

I was beginning to get quite skilled at investing money on a short-term basis to attract the maximum interest, and the bank must have been fed up with my frequent phone calls to ask: 'What is the rate in Jersey today?' We were accumulating enough money to invest but we were also beginning to accumulate another problem. We no longer had sufficient room, even with Brookfield Farm, to cope with all the donkeys that were coming in. We had worked hard on our rehabilitation scheme and we now had 116 donkeys out on rehabilitation. As fast as we got the donkeys into good homes the early ones we had sent out seemed to come back and it was very difficult to make any real impact on our numbers. Frequently horse-owners rang up asking if they could have a donkey to keep their horse company and we agreed to this because the donkeys seemed to enjoy the company of another equine and it worked very well. However, donkeys that had been out keeping horses company began to start coming back more and more frequently. On checking up through our inspectors we found that the owners of the horses were being told by their veterinary surgeons that it was dangerous to keep a donkey with a horse as donkeys were silent carriers of lungworm parasites.

Whilst these didn't affect the donkey much, according to the vets, they could be fatal to the horses. This piece of news was extremely disturbing and we determined to start some work on the project to see if this was indeed the case. We worked through various surveys and current research work that had been done and found that much of the problem had arisen over the mis-identification of the lungworm larva, which was very similar to certain gut larvae. Niels, with his degree in biology and botany, was extremely interested in this and he found out that a great deal of research had been carried out on cattle but little on donkeys because of the expense. Apparently the donkey could be a host to the lungworm and not show symptoms because of lack of exertion, but it was doubtful if anyone had successfully indenti-fied the lungworm larva. It was decided that we would obtain three or four horses that we were sure were clear of lungworm and use them for the follow-up research work.

First, we would identify the proper larvae. Second, we would see if the larva was the same in the horse as the donkey. Third, we would see whether there was any cross between the two.

Niels decided to set up a laboratory using the cellars of our house, to which all the trustees and the veterinary surgeons agreed, provided that no donkey was put to inconvenience, pain or suffering whatsoever. The programme was arranged so that the donkey was involved in no more than its droppings being picked up. We found, when the project had started, that the veterinary department of Glasgow University was extremely interested in the work that we were doing; both Niels and I flew up to Glasgow to meet Hilary Clayton of the university, who was engaged in a large project specifically to prove the incidence of lungworms in horses and donkeys. It was a most interesting liaison. The veterin-ary hospital at the university was of course fascinated that we had

148

so many donkeys with such meticulous records, and they helped by providing special anthelmintics and introducing us to various chemical firms who were manufacturing drugs to prevent lungworm. By a little persuasion we were able to get all our dosing supplied free. This work was linked with the work being done by IDPT and gradually we began to build up a picture of the donkeys' problems, not only from our own large numbers but on a wider basis from the rest of the world.

I had always hated the thought of any experiments on live animals, and since the arrival of Mollie Bunday, with her terrible history, I had been very worried by chemical firms carrying out experiments on animals. A lady in Kent had written saying that Burroughs Welcome were carrying out experiments using donkeys and ponies in a chemical works near to her home. I decided to investigate and rang Burroughs Welcome direct. It wasn't easy to get through to the right person and they were very wary of my request to speak to the person concerned with the donkeys. Eventually I got hold of the director of this department and he invited me to visit the research laboratory to see what was taking place. With some trepidation I went. The donkeys being used were kept in a large barn similar to ours at Slade House Farm. I am quite sure that the facilities there had not been specially prepared for my visit. They had a deep bed of clean straw, plenty of hay and water. All the donkeys were very fit and well and all came up to me with no sign of fear or of being mistreated. The purpose of these donkeys was to provide a blood supply for making plasma for treating sick animals. It was rather like the blood donors scheme carried out on humans. I can't say I liked the idea but it was quite apparent that the donkeys didn't suffer in any way. They assured me that all the donkeys were kept until old age, when they were humanely put down and then bled out. They showed me photographs of the condition of the donkeys as they arrived and they were probably better off being kept in these ideal conditions than in the dealers' yards from which they had come, or even than working on the beaches.

Experimentation on animals is an extremely emotive problem and I think in the end I justified it in my own mind in that they were in fact helping their own kind and there was certainly no sign of any ill-treatment of any sort from Burroughs Welcome.

On 8 June 1977 Arthur Negus and his wife visited the sanctuary. It was a very special day for us. They were such charming people and they fell in love with a little donkey who had arrived at the sanctuary the day before and was as yet unnamed. He was promptly named Negus and we were given a cheque sufficient to pay for his keep for a year.

My daughter Lise was getting married in July and Niels having launched his boat was sailing madly every single weekend. By now I had given up any pretence of being able either to sail or go to church at the weekends. We were all under great pressure outside as every box seemed to be full and no sooner did we get donkeys cleared of their four-week isolation period than once again another load would come in and we would be in trouble again. The RSPCA at Blackpool did a wonderful job with one of the beach owners. He retired one of his donkeys at the end of each year and Inspector Matthews there would ring up the sancturary and we would go down and collect those going into retirement. They were beautiful animals and although elderly always in excellent condition.

The majority of them were very large donkeys and one called Buffalo was the largest donkey ever to come into the sanctuary. He had the most enormous feet and his ears must surely have been the biggest in the business. They were so big that he had a great job to hold them upright and would normally stand with both ears drooping, either over the side of his face or down towards his nose. He loved standing at the gate meeting people as he was very, very sociable and you only had to call his name and the two enormous ears would raise up to their full position and his profile has to be seen to be believed.

June 1977 seemed to be a month of great events. David Way, the producer of the Angela Rippon programme *Peninsula*, called to discuss the idea of doing a half-hour programme on the Donkey Sanctuary. He was a charming man and spent almost the whole day going round the sanctuary talking to me and discussing plans for the programme. Angela Rippon had always been a great lover of horses and her attention had been drawn to the work of the sanctuary. He got extremely enthusiastic and although I could see we were going to have to spend a great deal of time coping with camera crews to make a film I felt it would be in the best interests of the sanctuary if we were to do this and so we agreed that they would come and film at a later date.

The day following the producer's visit we received a telephone call from *Animal Magic* to say that they would like to do a programme and we went through almost the same day's discussion with the producer from that. They were all very interested in the work and it seemed that the sanctuary was going to be famous at last.

At one of Niels' meetings in Exeter he had met Pam Goodger, the publicity officer for Longleat House, owned by the Marquess of Bath's family. She had talked to Niels extensively about our work and followed this up by an invitation to meet the Marquess of Bath at Longleat House to talk in particular about our work with the handicapped children. Niels and I went up to see them and were treated like royalty. Longleat House is such a magnificent building and it was beautiful to see the original rooms in use behind the scenes for the day-to-day running of Longleat. They made us the most exceptional offer. They offered us the free use of their grounds for a peak Sunday the following July to hold an event to raise funds for the Slade Centre. We couldn't turn this offer down, it was such a magnificent chance as they have approximately 8,000 people a day going through their gates on Sundays, and so after a most interesting day we returned home to work out how we could best make use of their tremendous offer for the handicapped children.

11 The Slade Centre

My dream of bringing health and happiness to handicapped children with the aid of donkeys had come at a difficult time. The move to Slade House Farm was imminent and I was very fully involved for the next few months and unable to take the project much further. A visit from a group of small handicapped children to the donkey sanctuary, however, stung me into action.

We had been asked by Millwater School of Honiton, which caters for educationally subnormal children, if a few children could be brought up for a visit, and one afternoon Mr George Hopkins, the headmaster, his wife and a few of the staff brought along some of their pupils. The nursery box at that time had some extremely gentle donkeys in it including My Poppett, Jess and Bilko, and a very pathetic donkey called Maundy, who had come in with the most appalling feet, and who had given birth to a dear little foal which we named Fay. We allowed the handicapped children to talk to them through the gate and after a few moments, as the donkeys were behaving so beautifully, I allowed the children in. The reaction of both children and donkeys was wonderful. Some of the children were affected mentally, others physically and mentally, but all of them found the most tremendous excitement and joy in being able to handle and cuddle the donkeys. The donkeys seemed to enjoy it equally and the very real cries of joy affected all the adults watching. I just sat there and reflected – was this what I had been working towards? It

was magical and so worth while to see the satisfaction and fulfil-
ment the children got.

We had selected a few of our older, steadier donkeys and we
saddled three of these up to see if the children enjoyed being taken
for a ride. At first they screamed with terror as the donkeys began
to move but within a few minutes all but two were thoroughly
enjoying the experience. George Hopkins was equally as impressed and on the spur of the moment I asked if he would
become a trustee if I were to make my dream into a reality and
register a new charity for handicapped children. He gladly
agreed and from that second the project was really under way.

I wanted to choose my team of trustees very carefully and
selectively as this time the charity would be working amongst
educationalists as well as animal lovers. Niels at the hotel had
already been busy helping the handicapped; he had been
approached by a gentleman called David Miller, who was
employed by the social services in Honiton, and had allowed the
swimming pool to be used every Monday morning for the severely
handicapped swimming club which was named the Dolphins.
Niels and David Miller got on very well indeed and when I met
David it seemed that he could contribute a great deal; so he too
was invited to be a trustee. My sister Pat was another obvious
choice with her Froebel-trained degree, and once again June
Evers agreed to join us with her medical knowledge. Niels and
I together made up a body of six trustees with a fairly wide
experience and the first trustees' meeting was held on 12 August
1975.

It seemed important for this charity to have some well-known
patrons as we wanted the word to spread fast, and we were going
to need large sums of money to build the dream centre that I had
planned in my mind. We were already receiving generous donations from James Mason for the Donkey Sanctuary and wrote
first to him to see if he would become our main patron. We were
all delighted when he accepted and then at the suggestion of the
other trustees we drew up a list and were thrilled when people
accepted our invitations. They included Dorian Williams, Leslie
Crowther, Charlie Chester, Spike Milligan, Richard Hearne,
Bob Forbes, Dr Freddie Brimblecombe, and the Bishop of

Dunwich, Rev. T. H. Cashmore. Once again John Lovell was called upon to set up the charity and arrange for registration with the Charity Commission.

I had a good idea in my mind of what I wanted our centre to look like but I had been very interested to see an article in *The Pony* describing the Diamond Riding Centre which catered for ponies and disabled children in Surrey. The architect of that centre was Brian Drury and Niels and I rang him up and arranged to visit the centre. It was a most interesting day. Obviously the building was very much larger than we would need and included residential accommodation and the most enormous indoor arena and stable blocks but it immediately formulated our minds as to how the centre should be built and with the trustees' approval we asked Brian Drury to draw up plans to our specified needs.

We envisaged two distinct areas, one in which the children could play and be looked after between rides, and a large arena where they could actually have the rides. Attached to the arena would be an area for petting stables where the children could go and cuddle and talk to the donkeys in between their rides. And we wanted an observation room with one-way glass so that specialists and helpers watching the children's progress could observe the children without them feeling that beady eyes were on them all the time. It was essential that the maximum relaxation and pleasure should be given to the children.

We wanted special sprays so that the arena could be kept dampened down so that the asthmatic children wouldn't be affected by dust, overhead heating to keep them all warm and, if possible, a type of sound equipment that would enable the children to be talked to directly by the teacher in the observation room rather than by overhead loudspeakers. The idea really was for a children's haven, a day away from the rigidity of hospitals and hospital schools, where the luxury of normal living entered these children's days perhaps for the first time.

We didn't want the bright reds, blues and yellows of primary colours that the children were used to, we wanted subtler, more relaxing shades of paintwork and decoration throughout the centre, the whole atmosphere to be one of enjoyment and pleasure and above all a change of environment that even the most handicapped child could appreciate. So many extremely handicapped children are never able to leave their hospital schools because there are simply not the facilities at the places they wish to visit. A special medical room was planned with full changing facilities for children and even a bath for emergencies. And then there were kitchens where the helpers could make their much-needed cups of tea and children could be given drinks too.

Brian Drury drew up the plans to our joint specifications. We then turned to estimating how many schools we could help and what the potential was in the local area.

George Hopkins and I drew up a list of schools for the handicapped within a thirty-mile radius, and a simple questionnaire was designed and sent to find out whether or not the schools would like the opportunity of coming to our centre if it were to be built and to find out the degree of handicaps from each school to whom we were writing.

The head teachers from all schools were invited to an informal evening at Slade House Farm and I got an immense boost when eleven schools were represented. The encouragement they gave us was wonderful. In the area there were apparently difficulties in finding extra activities their children could take part in as indeed it seems there is all over the country and for hospital schools like Franklyn Hospital School at Exeter, and Courtenay Hospital School at Stoke Lyne, Exmouth, one of their biggest problems in taking their children out anywhere was finding somewhere which had the proper facilities for the care of their severely physically and mentally handicapped children. A lot of these children had regular epileptic fits so they were thrilled with our promise of beds and even baths for their more difficult cases.

And so the idea of our centre, which could possibly incorporate all these items, was of the greatest interest to them. But to make sure we were working along the right lines five of us started taking a team of our donkeys round to five of the schools for one morning or afternoon each week so that we could gauge the value of the whole project before anything further was spent.

Noddy, who loved to get away from the household chores, had always been extremely keen on horses, and she and I together gathered up a team of donkeys that we thought suitable and

155

organized our first visits. My mother hated being left alone at this time and so she came with us and would sit looking after the riding hats which she passed out to each child. We found the children absolutely loved her and one large angular boy at the Courtenay Hospital School wandered up to her and said, 'Are you a real granny?' and she said, 'Yes, dear.' 'I have never met a real granny before,' he said. 'Can I kiss you?' And this poor handicapped child bent down and kissed my mother firmly.

The arrival of the donkeys in their specially adapted horse-box became to some children the most important time of the week. With a team of voluntary helpers from the neighbourhood we would drive into the hospital schools and park the lorry near the area we had chosen to work in. The joy on the children's faces as the donkeys came down the ramp was indescribable. Some of the children were so handicapped or crippled that it took two grown men to carefully lift them on to the backs of the donkeys. It took three helpers to each donkey, one to lead and two to support the child on each side, and our first visits to the different schools were always extremely difficult. Our weight regulations were very carefully maintained and no child over eight stone was allowed a ride.

Some of the children screamed as soon as they saw the donkeys, but others would run up and throw their arms round them and gain tremendous comfort from the close association with such a large woolly animal. I can't describe the donkeys' behaviour but it was somewhere near miraculous. Children would scramble under the donkeys' tummies and the donkeys would stand there patiently looking down with a kindly glance. We tried to teach the children from the start the correct side to mount and never to go behind a donkey and even to some of these pathetic little cases the message gradually got through. By the time we had visited each school five or six times on a regular basis almost every child greeted the arrival of the donkeys with squeals of joy.

I formulated a theory then which I still believe, that the child looked on the donkey as a handicapped horse. For some reason people seem to laugh at donkeys and perhaps they felt a liaison that they too were not quite right and were also laughed at, at times. Whatever the link it was certainly there and when the plans for our riding centre were proposed by Brian Drury I knew the money somehow had to be found to build the centre.

With the trustees we sat down to work out the best way of introducing our scheme to the planning authorities to produce the quickest result. Suddenly the winter was upon us, the joy of taking the donkeys to the children was over and we realized that the indoor centre was urgently needed. We were so afraid that the progress we were making with the children was going to be lost and the trustees decided to invite the Chief Planning Officer, Mr Dixon, to advise us which site to select. He came and on 26 August 1975 walked around and seemed extremely impressed by the idea of the whole project, although he did say there could well be some planning problems as the sanctuary is situated in an area of outstanding natural beauty and a coastal preservation area and we wanted the Slade Centre near by.

But still full of enthusiasm, I took the plans to Mr Howarth of the Sidmouth town council and began to feel the first inkling of the trouble that was to lie ahead. Our local paper, the *Sidmouth Herald*, was right behind us and on 30 August they produced a special feature outlining the idea for the Slade Centre. I just couldn't believe the headline that appeared two weeks later in the same paper.

DONKEY PLAN LOOKS LIKE BITING THE DUST

Mrs Elisabeth Svendsen's idea for a riding centre for disabled children at the Donkey Sanctuary, Slade House Farm, Salcombe Regis, looks like biting the dust before she has even made formal application to the East Devon District Council.

Mrs Svendsen discussed her plans with Mr Eric G. Howarth, Clerk of Sidmouth Town Council, and last week he mentioned them to members of the Planning Committee.

After a long discussion the committee decided unanimously to oppose Mrs Svendsen's idea.

The decision was based partly on strong opposition from the Sid Vale Association, but mostly on the feelings of councillors that the proposals would be completely out of keeping with the area of outstanding natural beauty in which the farm is set.

Among the council members who opposed the plan was Mr S. N. Baker, himself a disabled person, who said, 'Everyone has a great deal

157

of sympathy with a scheme like this, but on the site proposed it is just not on.'

Councillor C. E. Fryer, Chairman of Sidmouth Town Council, said he was sure most members of the public would feel the centre should be allowed, but on planning grounds there were many reasons for turning it down.

Although members of the Planning Committee seem adamant in their opposition to the proposal, no definite decision has been taken. This is because the plans have not yet been formally put before the council.

And even when they have been, the Town Council can make only a recommendation which may be overruled by the East Devon District Council.

Mrs Svendsen's reaction to the council's attitude was one of bitter disappointment.

She said, 'I cannot understand why this plan should meet with such fierce opposition. The proposed riding school would be behind the present farm buildings and down in a dip. It would not be visible from the road or the coastal walk. People would have to go out of their way to find it. I am not a property shark trying to make thousands of pounds by speculating on tower blocks which will ruin the countryside. One of the reasons my husband and I live in this area is because we love the beautiful scenery, so why should we want to spoil it?

'Since we moved the Donkey Sanctuary to Slade House Farm earlier this year, we have made improvements to its appearance. We are currently engaged in an extensive tree-planting scheme in partnership with the Men of the Trees.

'Why should handicapped children not be able to share in the beauty we all appreciate so much, and have some really worthwhile therapy at the same time? If my plans are turned down, it will be a great disappointment, not only to me, but to dozens of needy children in this area. There must be a way to work this out so everyone is happy.'

I just couldn't believe that before we had even submitted the plans they'd been turned down. Since our arrival at Slade House Farm we had improved it greatly and we had reduced traffic to the area by closing the caravan park and stopping the letting of the holiday flats. Amongst the number of letters that appeared the next week supporting our idea there were an equal number opposing it, and the wildest accusations and suggestions began to be published in the press. We were taking the food from the mouths of dying children starving in Bangladesh, and it was just another way of getting planning permission for a holiday camp. Of course our biggest opponents of all were the Sid Vale Association, set up to protect the natural amenities of Sidmouth and its surrounding area and they were certainly a force to be reckoned with.

There is no doubt that the planners and ourselves were put under the greatest possible pressure. With the architect we had chosen a site which we knew could not be seen from anywhere and which blended in with the buildings already around the farm. Had we been of agricultural status we would have been allowed to erect a barn much higher than the building we proposed with no planning permission needed at all and yet we were willing to raise the funds to help children in desperate need in our own locality by building our centre, and were receiving almost fanatical opposition.

Many people, particularly from the horse world, were not sure that donkeys were the right animals to do the job. Pony riding for the disabled had proved valuable but I felt convinced that the gentler donkey also had a great deal to offer since not only is it easier for a child to obtain the correct riding position on the narrower back of the donkey compared to the pony but the whole animal is much more cuddly, warm and attractive to the child. Having once got used to riding on our donkeys the child could go on to riding ponies with a distinct advantage.

I also knew that most of the riding for the disabled centres were only open for half a day a week and our donkeys were already in demand for many more sessions than we could fulfil, even going out five times a week.

The plans were officially submitted and the letters and the arguments on the planning continued over Christmas. No decision had been made and the East Devon planners were being inundated by letters from our patrons, with people such as James Mason, Richard Hearne, Dorian Williams and the Vicar of Salcombe Regis, Michael Courtney, supporting us. It was decided that the planners would come out and see the site and make a decision after that.

It was a very tense day for us all. The planning committee

turned up in force and it was difficult to know who was on which side. All the questions were answered fully, and we appealed to them all for the sake of the handicapped children to support our application. In January the East Devon District Council eventually decided against us by twelve votes to seven. One member of the council said that he had turned down the application in the interest of the handicapped children and I think this hit me harder than anything else.

I just couldn't face anybody. I lay on my bed and cried. The rain was beating against the windows as I thought of the many handicapped children. They would have to wait until the summer not only this year but every other year. We just had to have that decision reversed.

In my dreams I had never considered anybody opposing the idea, and in a strange way I felt very sorry for the people responsible. Few of the actual members of the Sid Vale Association seemed to have been born and bred in Sidmouth; the majority had moved in from other parts of the country and had built their own modern bungalows or houses or moved into buildings which previous planners had seen fit to grant. I would invite the officials of their society up to see the site for themselves, take them round and appeal to them to reconsider their strong opposition.

A strong cup of coffee and some sensible words from Niels soon put me back on my feet and we called a trustees' meeting to plan our next action. We had just purchased Brookfield Farm and decided to put in a new planning application for the centre to be built there. The farm was miles from anywhere and at least the Sid Vale Association would not be able to put their force behind the opposition. Brian Drury had to go out and redraw all the plans. I think he was as disappointed as we were since he had spent a lot of time and effort in trying to get the plans passed, but he gladly started work at the new site.

In the meantime we started our second year's work in the summer of 1976 going out with the donkeys. The children had looked forward to this and waited anxiously for the weather to improve so that work could start. Our donkeys, including Solo and Black Coffee, remembered their way round the hospitals and schools so well that they hardly needed any leaders. Solo enjoyed more than anything going up the long ramp and into one of the classrooms at Ellen Tinkham School near Exeter where the severely handicapped children would lie on airbeds, unable to come out into the garden unless the weather was particularly good. Solo would nuzzle up to them gently and the children would get the greatest pleasure from touching her soft nose and feeling the warmth of donkey's breath so close to them. The team that took the donkeys, led by Noddy, got tremendous pleasure and satisfaction from the trips, and the schools, who had originally thought it was going to be just another charitable idea which would fade out had now begun to realize that we really meant to continue the work, and were cooperating very fully.

We received the most marvellous letter from the headmistress of one of the schools as follows:

22 July 1976

Dear Mrs Svendsen,

I am writing on behalf of the staff and myself to thank you all so very much for bringing the donkeys to our school this term.

We must admit that the first Thursday you came it was all great fun for the children – but we honestly thought that you and your helpers were living in cloud cuckoo land, with your records of progress and mounting and sitting and the other things you asked us to do. All the staff wish me to tell you how very wrong we were – the progress of so many of the children has really amazed us – the different way they now sit and how so many of them can now sit without support. Tim who is so spastic has now got the idea of sitting up. The joy the rides bring to blind, very sub-normal James, the real laughter that comes from those who very seldom laugh. Perhaps the greatest thing to us is the motivation it has given to Stephen – for three years we have tried to find something to motivate this very withdrawn little boy who lives in a world of his own – the first day we saw him climb on the donkey – on his own – well we could have cried. I don't think you and your great band of helpers quite realize the good you have done to these severely sub-normal, multiply handicapped children.

We cannot thank you enough and beg you to try to keep coming – you must know the importance of continuity for these children.

So from all the children – the staff and myself we send you a very big thank you.

(signed) P. M. Dalaigh

No sooner had the plans been put in to Honiton for consideration for the new area when opposition started yet again. A petition was drawn up in a local village and David Miller, one of our trustees, who lived in Honiton, began to receive objectionable letters and phone calls, despite the fact that many Honiton children were already benefiting from the visits of the donkeys. A hasty trustees' meeting was called when the local parish council turned us down and as we knew the opposition was going to be extremely strong we decided to withdraw the application from East Devon planning meetings.

Niels was marvellous in his support at this time. 'Come on,' he said. 'It is not like you to give up. We'll start a new campaign in March and we will fight every inch of the way. We will organize our own petition and we will get the handicapped schools and children to help us and I am sure if we all pull together we can win through.'

It was like preparing for a battle. We already knew most of the objections that were going to be thrown at us and the first people I invited up were the chairman, secretary and treasurer of the Sid Vale Association. It was a pleasant meeting but they didn't seem at all impressed. All they could say was: 'This is an area of out-standing natural beauty and we don't really think it suitable for you to build a centre and have handicapped children here.' Intimating any further application would be opposed. I felt indignant afterwards; I hadn't even gained an inch for the project.

The official line of the East Devon District Council had been to recommend to the committee that the plans were passed and so they at least were on our side but there were many members of both the Sidmouth Town Planning Committee and the East Devon Planning Committee who were totally opposed to our project. In case by this stage they weren't fully aware of all that the charity was aiming for we drew up a letter pointing out all the points in our favour. We changed the plans as far as possible to meet their recommendations and put a desperate appeal for the support of readers into all the local press. And this is the letter that I designed:

The Slade Centre,
Slade House Farm,
Salcombe Regis,
Nr Sidmouth
Devon

Dear Reader,

This is a desperate appeal to you personally, to help us in our efforts to obtain planning permission to build an indoor centre for severely handicapped children. They will be brought, winter and summer, to love, enjoy and slowly learn the basic elements of riding, using our carefully trained and selected donkeys.

A special building is essential, for this work incorporates ramps for wheelchairs, guide rails for the blind, sprinklers to keep down dust in the arena area, special toilets for the handicapped and good heating facilities.

You may remember that our last application to build a centre at Slade House Farm was turned down by a very narrow majority under pressure from the Sid Vale Association. Having been turned down we felt that if the children could not come to us, we would go to the children, and this we did. The results of fifty-one sessions at five handicapped schools and hospitals within a twenty-mile radius has proved the immense value of the work, and written and pictorial evidence is available.

Some children, for the first time in their lives, actually began to count the days of the week, because, for them, one day was 'Donkey Day'. Their disappointment when the weather stopped our regular visits affected the school and hospital staff, as well as us. We wait to see how much of the immense progress made has been retained by the children when we start again in the spring . . . How much better if we could bring them all out in our specially adapted coach (which could take wheelchair cases) every week. Facilities get less and less for them with the cutback in spending by local authorities, and this would be totally charitable, neither the children, schools, hospitals or education authorities being asked to provide one penny.

In deference to the Sid Vale Association, we applied for planning permission to build the centre at Farway, at our new farm. Imagine our disappointment when this was turned down by the local Parish

Council. We had to think again, and the Trustees decided that if we re-designed it to suit the Planning Committee, and to meet as far as possible the requests of the Sid Vale Association, we might be able to have it at Slade House Farm. After all, last year Sidmouth Town Council passed the plans and everyone was surprised when the East Devon District Council Planning Committee ignored the recommendation of their own site inspection committee, and turned the plan down by a small majority.

We agree that we are in an 'area of outstanding natural beauty' but then so is quite a large area of Devon: over 300 square miles of it!

WHY STOP HANDICAPPED CHILDREN ENJOYING IT? THE FACTS ARE AS FOLLOWS:

1 The new building will be built on agricultural lines, redesigned from the last application to fit in with the planners' requirements.

2 This time no accommodation will be provided, therefore, if necessary the building could revert to agricultural use, and this could be a condition of the consent.

3 The building can NOT BE SEEN FROM ANYWHERE, as agreed by last year's site committee, so it is hard to see how it can spoil the neighbourhood.

4 The maximum height of the building will be sixteen feet, lower than the average house, and very much lower than Slade House Farm itself.

5 Did you know that up until last year there was a licensed caravan site at Slade House Farm? This was closed by the Sanctuary, thus reducing traffic. Our coach and the volunteer helpers' cars will produce less traffic per day than the previous caravans.

6 Donkeys have proved ideally suitable for the task, and a trained riding instructress will be in charge of the riding. When the children grow too large, they can go on with confidence to riding ponies.

We all pray that to save the time and expense of an appeal, our local community will support us and help persuade the Planning Committee to make a favourable decision this time on the centre so that we can commence it in JUBILEE YEAR, in deference to Her Majesty's wishes that projects should be concerned with young people. We hope to call it 'THE SLADE JUBILEE CENTRE'.

If YOU want our local handicapped children to be able to use this centre then please help us by voicing YOUR opinion, either by signing

a petition in favour of the project, or by writing to East Devon District
Council direct.

c/o Mr A. S. Dixon, Chief Planning Officer
East Devon District Council
31 Southernhay East, Exeter EX1 1NT

Once again the press went to town. Letter after letter and article
after article appeared for and against the project. The planning
meeting was to be in May 1977 and over 1,328 people signed our
petition. We arranged a demonstration outside the planning
meeting and every councillor arriving was greeted by donkeys and
handicapped children. When the last councillor had arrived Niels
and I and all our supporters slipped into the public benches,
filling them to capacity. On the other side of the public section
could be seen the Sid Vale delegation, sitting every bit as tensely
as we were. I nearly cried as Councillor Ernest Whitton stood up
and supported us strongly and we sat with baited breath while
the vote was taken. It was approved by fifteen to three.

However, there were conditions, one being that we would
almost have to redesign the whole centre to meet the planners' requirements. But redesign we would and submit the plan to the
council again before we could actually start our work.

The planning troubles almost solved, finance became the next
headache. An enormously encouraging thing had happened –
the Tiverton Youth Centre organized a sponsored walk and I
went over with one of the little donkeys to meet them at the
end of the gruelling ordeal. They raised over £300 for the Slade
Centre and this was the first substantial sum we received. I had
been told by the Charity Commission of a special book called
Directory of Grant-making Trusts, listing many charitable trusts
willing to give money to projects like ours. We wrote over two
hundred letters to obtain funds but the response was extremely
disappointing; why did it seem so much easier to raise money for
the donkeys that it was for the handicapped children? However,
after the battles we'd already had we just kept on writing and the
money began to come in.

Our original estimate on the cost of the building had been
between £80,000 and £90,000 but now, to our horror, with the

passage of time this had increased to between £130,000 and £140,000. This figure seemed impossible in view of my poor efforts in raising funds. It was also extremely expensive employing an architect from such a long distance and very regretfully and on the best of terms we decided we would have to change our architects.

A firm of architects in Exeter drew up all the plans anew. We made the centre slightly smaller and adapted it to the planners' requirements. We also managed to get the price of the centre down to a more manageable £75,000 and our new plans were passed without too much problem. The foundation stone was laid on 14 June 1978.

Once again we went out to the schools during that summer and by now the children were the greatest of friends with us. It was very sad to find that some of the children with progressive diseases had in fact sunk backwards and were unable to get the same benefit from the donkeys as the year before but this was made up for by the many children who had now improved to such an extent that they could ride unaided with only a helper leading the donkey.

In the three years since we had started going out to the schools some of our original pupils had now grown too large and it was heartbreaking to see their disappointment when they were unable to ride. However, I had a little trap and Noddy and I dusted it down and altered it so that we could lift the handicapped children up into it when they were too large to actually ride the donkeys. It also took the children who were too handicapped for riding. This proved a great success and we decided to tarmac a track round the actual Slade Centre so that the children could drive round in the traps. The planners had asked us to make a high bank to obscure the centre from the main road and we made this wide enough to possibly use one day in the future so that the children would get a superb sea view from above the centre.

Staffing of the new project had to be thought about. Noddy had left us to be near her ageing mother in Cornwall. My sister Pat, a fully qualified teacher, was finding life lonely as a widow at Compton Dando. At a trustees' meeting she was approved as the supervisor in charge of the play area section and decided on two qualified riding instructors to run the riding part. Obviously salaries could not be high and Pat agreed to come in at a salary of approximately half that she was receiving as a teacher. It was a tremendous weight off my mind when I knew Pat could come and run the centre because without totally dedicated staff projects of this sort cannot continue. Pat was totally dedicated, not only to the donkeys but to children as I was and her very real enthusiasm would, I knew, really get Slade going.

The offer from the Marquess of Bath had been gratefully accepted and we got together with the Donkey Breed Society who very helpfully agreed to put on a donkey show on the date selected, all funds going to the Slade Centre. The sanctuary had already agreed that it would make it a very special day to show off the donkeys and all the work being done at Slade House Farm and with Julie's organizing ability from the office we commenced the mammoth task of organizing tents, show rings and catering facilities for the thousands we hoped would arrive. We spent weeks of preparation and work and on the great day the enormous marquee was full of donkeys and goods to buy. The Donkey Breed Society had organized a superb show which included fancy-dress classes which were already fully subscribed, a large number of our handicapped children taking part. We had organized three busloads of children from our schools and all seemed set for the most wonderful fund-raising event.

James Mason and Arthur Negus had agreed to be there and you can imagine our horror when tremendous gale-force winds hit the site the night before and the day was marred by torrential rain. Over 4,000 visitors did, however, turn up to see us and the work done at the Donkey Sanctuary and in aid of the children and we were lucky to get away without making a substantial loss. The Marquess of Bath and his family were absolutely wonderful to us and he presented us with a superb coat of arms to be given to the child who made the most progress in each year at the Slade Centre.

I missed Niels desperately at this time as he was battling his way round Britain on the Round Britain Race with his partner, Norman Brook. He was very sad not to be there and I could certainly have done with his shoulder to lean on when we realized that the day had not turned out the financial success we had hoped. However, there was no doubt that 4,000 more people knew of the work we were doing.

We had always assumed that the children could be brought in from the schools by their own school buses but it soon became apparent that this was not going to be the case. We needed our own bus, one with a hydraulic lift at the back for the wheelchairs and stretcher children and with room to place those children who had to be carried on airbeds in a comfortable position. We eventually designed and ordered our bus which was going to cost £9,000 and take six months to build but I must admit, as the time came near for payment and delivery of the bus for the official opening on 5 December, I was getting a little desperate. One of the foundations I had written to in the book of charity trusts had been the Llankelly and Hambland Foundation and they came up trumps with a magnificent cheque for £9,000, received shortly before the bus was delivered.

We had to provide lunch for some of the children as their school arrangements just didn't fit. The average cost for a school meal turned out to be 75p and Niels promised that the hotel would provide lunches at this cost but, of course, of a slightly different standard to that achieved perhaps in hospital schools. Mrs Pitts of the School Meal Service helped tremendously, providing special heat-insulated boxes to transport the hot food.

The day of 5 December was cold but bright and in a very moving opening ceremony, which was performed by the Marquess of Bath, the Slade Centre was opened and ready to start work.

The beautiful big play area that we built had been furnished by the kindness of many companies who had donated toys and furnishings to us. In particular the Relyon group donated play furniture and Piccolo Books keep us supplied with a complete children's library. The problem of giving rides to children in wheelchairs had always been with us and I rang Westland Helicopters one day to see if they could suggest any way of making a special donkey trap into which we could put a wheelchair with a child in it. They took up the project with their second-year engineering students and built the most magnificent cart in which

168

the back lets down, ramps come out, and the wheelchair is simply pushed up the back and strapped into place, the back ramp being the back of the trap when fastened up.

Around the centre is the tarmac track for cart-riders and our riding instructors have designed a beautiful set of traffic lights which the children have to obey, also the stop and go sign in the hope of trying to instil some form of road safety into the lesson. Having the indoor centre has meant that we have been able to progress with some of the schools to the first stages of a proper riding lesson.

The centre is open six days a week and fifty weeks a year as, of course, handicapped hospital schools do not take normal school holidays. A team of forty *crème de la crème* donkeys has been specially selected for the work at Slade and the team thoroughly enjoys itself. Ten donkeys are on duty for a week at a time and have three weeks off so none can be even remotely overworked and it is surprising how they line the rails of the paddock in which they are kept as the school bus arrives each day and genuinely enjoy the shouts and yells of the visiting children as they see their favourites.

The staff at Slade are showing complete dedication to their job and the love and enthusiasm that manifests itself throughout the whole of the Slade Centre is immediately apparent to visitors and staff alike and makes completely worth while the years of effort in establishing Slade, one of the most unique riding centres in existence. It has now been open for nearly two years.

The summer of 1977 and the sailing season were in full swing. Niels, often accompanied by Clive, was racing regularly and my weekends became busier and busier and tended to be rather lonely. Saturday nights always seemed the worst and June, Sarah and I would try and make up expeditions, collecting fossils on the beach at Lyme Regis being one of our favourite trips, or going with our dogs for long walks along the cliffs.

Rosie arrived from near Pontefract, and hers was a very sad story. The girl who brought her was a French student teacher and she wrote us a pathetic letter saying that 'they wanted to get rid of the donkey and I wanted to buy it for several reasons. If it were mine I would be able to have her hooves cut which they have not done for more than six months and it is a terrible sight. They are as long as a pair of shoes curling up in the air. Once its feet were walkable I would be able to take it out from its stable as it never goes out, it lives in a tiny hole. If you will take it from me I will get it. I hate to think they might sell her tonight and push her half crippled into the butcher's van for meat. She is standing day and night in a little corner isolated from the outside by a window covered by a plastic sheet. Please help.'

We couldn't ignore this cry and our fears were realized when Rosie arrived as she looked even worse than we had imagined. Sadly we were too late to help her. Her feet had not been treated for over four years in our estimation and she had been totally deprived of any exercise for at least six months. We slowly started to feed her up and walked her gently each day and she was given a large airy stable, but the damage had already been done and she died in November.

We were more fortunate with little Tinkerbell. She arrived as a pathetic eight-month-old filly, her mother's condition as desperate as her own. She was very elderly and heavily in foal. Both were covered in lice and sores but our attempts here were rewarded and both recovered fully.

Our first taste of TV film crews came with the *Animal Magic* unit. For three days the whole sanctuary was disrupted, almost all our time totally taken up by the demands of producer and cameraman. We would just get all the donkeys in exactly the right place that everybody liked and myself just ready to start or continue an interview, when the sun would go in, or the sound of an aeroplane would intrude and we all had to stop and wait until all the crew was satisfied. I never realized it would take so long to make a film that only showed for four minutes.

Our next film crew was for the Angela Rippon *Peninsula* programme and this proved very much easier. I am not sure whether or not we had all got more used to the idea now and knew what would be wanted of us but it certainly seemed to flow much more easily and in two days they had canned enough film for a half-hour programme. Angela Rippon herself was absolutely marvellous. I had always thought I was full of energy but I found myself rushing to keep up with her as she went round the sanctuary finding the next ideal site for a new shot. She was totally involved with the work we were doing and even when off film would be asking me questions about the donkeys and their welfare. She really had a genuine love of all the animals and I am sure this came across in the programme. There was one scene when we were in the main yard with all the geriatric donkeys and as usual Bimbo was standing with his head resting on my shoulder totally ignoring the active film crew. Angela was asking me why I cared so much for these old donkeys, and as I tried to describe my feelings when I used to have to sit up all night with sick donkeys and the way I tried to justify the existence of the human beings who had caused the donkeys to be in such desperate straits, my mind cast back to my night spent with poor Zebedee, who had eventually died. My eyes filled with tears and I found it difficult to continue. The camera, however, kept on rolling, and I had to pull myself together. It had obviously affected Angela Rippon as well and we had quite a job to finish that part of the interview. When it was over I asked Angela Rippon if she would re-do it as I was embarrassed at my obvious emotions. The team agreed and we managed to do the whole session without any breakdown. When the actual film came out, however, they had used the first part so the second take had been in vain.

171

By sheer coincidence the two programmes came out on the same night. The Angela Rippon report was a *Peninsula* programme and only shown in the South West, but the moment the programmes were over telephones started to ring and I was inundated by offers of help, including some very substantial promises of donations, which all transpired. Later we were approached by *Magpie*, the children's programme, and once again received a television crew with Jenny Handley doing the interviewing. She too proved interested and sympathetic to our cause and I think our donkey helpers enjoyed her presence more than any other. She had a superp figure; I don't think the Donkey Sanctuary staff have ever been so eager to help on a filming expedition as during the *Magpie* film!

We particularly emphasized the educational aspect of the work that we were doing on this programme and tried to educate the children who'd be watching as much as possible, including in the programme the work our farrier and vet do daily.

The most recent television crew to visit was the *Go with Noakes* team, as John Noakes was sailing round Britain and calling in at various interesting places. I think Shep was somewhat surprised to find so many donkeys and we had to be rather careful where he was allowed to run as donkeys are not particularly good with dogs. For the next few days after the filming the sanctuary rang with cries of 'Get down, Shep.'

The response to the Angela Rippon programme was fantastic. In view of the many letters received, the BBC decided to put the programme out again, this time nationally on BBC2 and a conservative estimate of funds raised by this second showing was in the region of £40,000. A further bonus was that the publishers Pan Books had seen and been deeply affected by our story. The editor of the children's books wrote to see if it would be possible for Pan to take over the four books that I had by now written for the sanctuary, but I felt that after already making such a good income for the sanctuary from the sale of these books we couldn't really let them go. To date over £39,000 has been contributed from the children's books to sanctuary funds. Pan Books then offered me a contract to write children's books for them, which I am now doing.

On 3 May Clive had his seventeenth birthday. We decided we would celebrate with a family outing to see the film *Abba*, which everybody was dying to see. We had received a donkey the day before called Moppett. She had come from a good home in the Midlands but her owners had lost the use of their field. This had proved disastrous and she had been moved from place to place until her owner found her heavily in foal and in desperate need of a permanent home. I was concerned, on this particular night, about Moppett as she seemed extremely uncomfortable and just as all the family was piling into the car ready for the outing I slipped into the isolation box where she was housed to check all was well. Immediately it was apparent that all was not well and Moppett was in deep distress. Rather miserably the family had to leave without me. I ran inside and rang the veterinary surgeon who agreed to come straight out. Moppett was lying down with her foal half presented but with the hind legs of the foal protruding instead of the forelegs. I knew it was going to be extremely tricky extricating the foal but the mare was in such distress that I daren't leave her any longer. It took twenty minutes to deliver the baby but at long last there was Moppett and the little foal called – what else? – Abba. Moppett stood herself up and shook herself and looked with some disgust at the wet little creature standing by her side. I moved the foal a little nearer to Moppett and thank goodness she began to lick it. As soon as the mare starts licking the foal it sets off a natural process which starts producing the mare's milk and this action is always the first sign that all is going to be well.

I was in quite a sorry state myself, the new dress I had put on for Clive's birthday was ruined, and I looked rather dismally at my filthy knees and arms. I'd just never stopped to think about what I was wearing. Moppett seemed fine and I began to go past her to get to the door of the stall to go out and have a bath. To my horror she suddenly lashed out with both back hooves and caught me a glancing blow on the thigh. I reeled backwards into the corner of the box and stood to see what she would do next. With her back end towards me she stood firmly between the door and myself. I was in somewhat of a predicament, to put it mildly, as every time I tried to move Moppett would make menacing movements with her back legs and it appeared I was firmly trapped in the corner until the family came back from the pictures. Then there was a sound out in the yard. It was the vet arriving and my shouts drew him to Moppett's box.

Between us we were able to distract her so that I could wriggle out from her stable. Now that she's got used to us she's the gentlest of donkeys and knows all our voices. Now wherever possible two of us always go into any new donkey's box.

Our biggest problem between the two farms was finding sufficient room to winter all the donkeys. They are not as hardy as many people imagine and to leave them out in the cold and wet through the winter months can be disastrous. We began to keep our eyes open for a suitable third farm which we could purchase. I was so lucky in the staff I had taken on. The office staff worked all the hours needed to get the work done and Julie was helping more than I could ever have believed. Gradually she was taking over the problems relating to the rehabilitated donkeys and it was a tremendous help to be able to delegate phone calls to her on this side of the project. She soon learnt how to protect me from the many cranky calls that we received and was wonderful in dealing gently with visitors who demanded in no uncertain terms that they must see Mrs Svendsen. The number of visitors was increasing each year and we had to provide two guides to take them round, partly for the visitors' sake but more importantly for the donkeys' sake to make sure no visitors fed them anything which was harmful. Despite our enormous notices of 'Please do not feed', people would try and give the donkeys the most unusual things and, of course, items such as meat and certain plants are poisonous to donkeys and even a carrot can prove disastrous with thirty donkeys in the same barn watching for it at the same time!

Quite recently we had taken a young donkey called Misty into the sanctuary. He had been bought by a kind and practical couple in Essex and they had given him plenty of attention, the trouble being that the more loving care he got the more he wanted. There were dogs and cats as company, but the dogs' company he disdained and the cats he delighted in chasing to show his contempt for them. He had not been gelded, which may have been one of

174

his difficulties and which led to him giving his owners the odd nip as they passed. Basically he was lonely and he had become a problem. When in his stable at night he misbehaved and, it seems, kept quite a few of the neighbours awake; to try and solve this problem his owners would leave him out in the field by the house if they had an evening engagement and leave the television on and the windows open so Misty could tune in. He stood with his jaw firmly resting on the railings, his eyes glued to the box and his ears pricked. The kindest thing seemed to take him into the sanctuary; now he's made a good friend of another of our donkeys, Maxi, has been gelded, and has learnt not to try to nip us as we pass by.

The writing of the newsletters continued apace as these proved so valuable not only to our fund-raising but in keeping everybody informed of what we are doing.

Lucky Lady and many of the older geriatric donkeys got very cold at night, despite their infra-red lamps and some kind people had knitted us some woollen blankets made from coloured squares which were joined together. The Angela Rippon programme had shown Lucky Lady with her blanket on and I put a small appeal in our newsletter for anybody who had time to knit one. Within a six-month period over 18,000 blankets arrived at the sanctuary and we are in fact extremely embarrassed at receiving so many. We thought of all the possible things we could do with them as there were many more than we could conceivably use and in the end we made a special arrangement with the Save the Children Fund to send our spare blankets that weren't suitable for donkeys to them and they in turn would help us on our journeys abroad by storing any items or drugs we needed for the donkeys which would help us greatly. Of course we had to tell people in the newsletter what we were doing and the many people who wrote offering to knit blankets were sent a copy of the 'knitters' news' which put the position to them before they started the blanket!

Outside, the dedicated workforce had risen in numbers under the watchful eye of John, and our veterinary surgeons were paying more and more visits each week. Every Monday was veterinary day and they would arrive and go round our two farms looking at all the donkeys we were concerned about and keeping a general eye on the running of the sanctuary from their professional viewpoint. They were extremely helpful and had helped set up the research programme into parasites. Approximately every second week we would have to take our stallions into their hospital at Exeter to be operated on and we found this a traumatic experience for the donkeys. It used to be a very long day as we would have to leave at seven thirty in the morning to have the donkeys settled down and ready for treatment by nine thirty a.m. We would allow them to rest as long as possible afterwards before starting the journey back to the sanctuary, and often we didn't arrive back until eight in the evening or after.

Dear Herb made the greatest friends with all the donkeys. His duty, after milking the cows in the morning, was to go round every donkey bathing its eyes to prevent any problems from flies. The very elderly donkeys tended to get sores resulting from the irritation caused by flies on their eyelids unless we cared for them on a daily basis and Herb was well known and loved by nearly every donkey. I think his greatest love was always Timothy, the donkey who had had his ears severed, and every day as Herb walked across the field Timothy would trot up to him and when Herb said, 'Good morning, Timothy, what about a handshake?' Tim would politely raise his left hoof and paw madly in the air until Herb took it and shook it firmly. I have a sneaking feeling that the donkeys' affection for Herb emanated from the endless supply of ginger biscuits that he carried around with him but it certainly did the job and he never had any problem catching a donkey to give it its treatment.

In 1978 we had a very cold winter indeed. The donkeys seemed to sense something was coming and there was a strange air of tension around the Donkey Sanctuary on Valentine's Day. One of our working staff was called Fred and on that particular morning he opened the gate to take the tractor through and to his horror, before he had time to close it again, a group of twenty-eight donkeys from the nursery group had squeezed through and set off at a gallop up the drive. Fred wasn't too concerned as the top gates are always kept tightly closed but as he walked up to

176

bring them back not a donkey was in sight and the top gates were wide open.

Fred rushed back to get his bicycle and without thinking to warn anybody else set off in pursuit of the twenty-eight. He obviously hadn't realized how fast the donkeys were going to travel. Niels and I were quietly having breakfast when we received a phone call from the Hare and Hounds pub a mile up the road. 'A group of your donkeys have just galloped past,' they said. 'There didn't seem to be anybody with them.'

Our breakfast forgotten, we rushed out to the door, jumped into the car and backed on to the little lane at the side of our house. Before Niels could put the car in forward gear a herd of donkeys galloped back across the lane in front of us and turned neatly back into the Donkey Sanctuary gates. All twenty-eight were there and beat Fred back to the sanctuary by a good twenty minutes! We all had a good laugh as we waited for Fred to come back panting.

The next morning we realized why they had been so keen to get some exercise – we woke up to a thick layer of snow. Snow in Devon is unusual and we all really quite enjoyed that first day. Even the donkeys seemed to like having a roll in it and we took the opportunity to take some movie films as we felt we might never see such a sight again. To our surprise, however, it snowed again the following day and the following day and by Saturday 18 February we had a full-scale blizzard raging. Niels was at the hotel and I was beginning to get a little apprehensive during the evening as there seemed to be at least two feet of snow outside our back door. June, Clive and I put on our ski anoraks and tried to walk up the main drive of the sanctuary to see how deep the snow was. The drifts were already approaching six feet deep and we had to turn back. We tried to make our way along the little lane to the main road but even these were blocked. To get back to the warmth of the house was wonderful.

I rang Niels and said, 'For heaven's sake get home as quickly as you can, darling, I think we are going to be snowed in.' Luckily he had taken the Land-Rover and he immediately set off home. It took him over two hours to get the six miles and he had to abandon the Land-Rover a quarter of a mile away on one of our lanes. He parked it behind a large Rolls-Royce which had also got stuck and left it thinking it would be easy to collect in the morning. By then we just couldn't believe it. The snow had drifted and been blown overnight to immense drifts of over fourteen feet deep. The lane where Niels had left his Land-Rover was part of the fields on either side and the only way you could tell where the lane was was by a major road ahead sign sticking out of the snow by the main road.

There wasn't a sound of a vehicle anywhere and we found ourselves totally cut off from the rest of the world. John Fry who lived next door and I with the children began the hard job of feeding the donkeys and reaching all the boxes. Luckily all were kept in and were warm but they weren't too pleased at having to wait for their breakfast. To our great joy Derek Battison who was supposed to be on duty that Sunday morning had made the tremendously dangerous journey of two miles from Salcombe Regis on foot, ploughing through drifts of between six and fourteen feet almost the whole way. We were very pleased to see him as obviously there was a great deal of work for us in caring for over 180 donkeys all trapped inside.

Derek had to move in with us for three days and as gradually one amenity after another failed and we sat with no hot water, no lights and rapidly getting short of food, he joined in the family games by candlelight and we all made the most of a very bad job. On the fourth day we put our skis on and skied down to Sidford to get bread not only for ourselves but for the other people trapped around us as it was physically impossible to move around without either skis or show shoes. It was certainly an experience none of us will forget and it was such a relief when the thaw came and we were able to move around again.

The severe cold proved too much for Lucky Lady and I was nearly heartbroken to find my old friend dead in her stable one morning. On the same day that she died another donkey called Old Lady came in so perhaps in a strange way it was Lucky Lady's replacement.

At the trustees' meeting held in February 1978 I pointed out the need to purchase new land as soon as possible as the number of donkeys in the sanctuary had risen to 494. We were absolutely at maximum capacity everywhere and none of us knew where to turn next. Paccombe House Farm, which was situated a mile and a half away, was coming up for auction that September and a visit proved that it would be absolutely ideal for us. It certainly wasn't farm land and previous farmers had got into trouble as much of the grassland was extremely rough and stretched away from the main farm at the bottom of the valley almost to the top of the valley, over 116 acres. It was, however, ideal for us and our desperate appeal for funds in the next newsletter to buy the farm enabled us to go to the auction with sufficient money to purchase.

Once again we were in trouble. The local press produced enormous headlines – 'Farmers protest over land for donkeys' – and the *Daily Mirror* headed its article 'No sanctuary! Slaughter old donkeys call' and wrote: 'A donkey sanctuary was lashed by angry farmers yesterday. They called for the old donkeys used by handicapped children for riding lessons to be killed as pet food.'

It really did seem that few local people liked our sanctuary. I found it very difficult to see their point of view, the land we had bought was not good farming land and when I thought how many millions of acres in this country had been turned over for agricultural use I really couldn't see why the donkeys should be deprived of this infinitesimal amount on which to spend their last days peacefully. We waited until the hue and cry had died down and then got on with the job of getting Paccombe ready for its new winter arrivals. There was a very large farmhouse which we divided into two. Derek Battison, who had been working with me now for over three years, was elevated to the position of manager and he and his wife and children moved into one side and Pat Feather, who was now working full time for Slade, moved into the other side.

Desperate efforts were made by all the staff and the large barns already on Paccombe Farm had their full complement of donkeys by the end of October. Christmas 1978 found us rescuing our worst group of donkeys yet, just when I was beginning to think things were easing up.

We were given news of fourteen donkeys in Hampshire who were in the deepest trouble. A lady living near realized the state of the animals and made collections locally to raise sufficient funds to buy them and send them to the sanctuary. I must admit that although my staff and I are used to appalling sights, we were all too upset to speak as the donkeys came down the ramp of the lorry. They were all absolutely saturated with rain and had been in a field with no hay or hard feed for some weeks. Two of the mares were heavily in foal and one had a tiny foal at foot whom we named Noel as it was so near Christmas. It was hard to tell he was white as on arrival he was so wet that he appeared thin and grey. He was beyond hope. Little Noel died but a tremendous fight began to save the lives of the other donkeys in the group and we succeeded. With the assistance of the RSPCA we hoped to bring a prosecution on the owner but unfortunately, due to witness difficulties and the time element, this proved impossible.

Just after they arrived Bernard Braden and his team came to make a programme on the sanctuary and they took some pictures of poor Jack, the stallion who had lost all the hair on his back due to the severe weather the donkeys had been exposed to. They were extremely interested not only in the sanctuary but also in the Slade Centre and the programme went out over the London region only. One day we are hoping this will be expanded to the whole country.

Every year in June Salcombe Regis holds the most enormous fair. Led by the church the whole village takes part and exhibitions of local crafts and the most beautiful flower display in the church hold pride of place. We were asked if we could provide a donkey or two with panniers to collect funds for the event and this we did gladly. The donkeys thoroughly enjoyed the day and raised a tremendous amount of money wandering up and down the little village streets whilst the milling crowds donated generously towards the fair.

We were calling on the vets more and more and the time was rapidly coming when it would be more economic to have our own veterinary surgeon. Andrew Trawford, a fully qualified vet who had previously been working with the Jamaican Society for the Protection of Animals and the Humane Society of Ontario in Canada, joined our executive team. A young enthusiastic veterinary surgeon, he welcomed the chance to concentrate on one species of animals, and donkeys, in particular, had always attracted him in Jamaica.

One winter night was quite an embarrassment. Niels and I had just gone to bed when I saw the outside lights had been left on. Clad only in Niels' pyjama jacket I went down the stairs and turned the latch on the back door as the light switch was at the top of the back stairs leading down to the sanctuary. I had my foot carefully in the door so that it would not slam but to my horror Tigger, my outside cat, made a mad dash to get into the kitchen for the night. Unthinkingly I withdrew my foot from the door and firmly put her at the top of the steps. You can imagine my horror when I turned round and found not only had I put Tigger out for the night but also myself. The door had locked behind me. At this stage I was not unduly alarmed as even though it was freezing cold I knew Niels was up in bed and would surely hear me banging the door and shouting. For over fifteen minutes I yelled, thumped, shouted and rang bells, but no Niels arrived and by this time I was getting chilly in certain areas to say the least.

I did not know whether to be pleased or not when I heard footsteps coming up to the back door; then Andrew appeared – he had seen the lights on in the yard and then heard my desperate yells and had come to help. I was trying to retain my dignity and talk to Andrew when the door from the flats opened and June arrived to see what all the noise and yelling was about. All three of us yelled and shouted together but to no avail. In the end I suddenly remembered that with June's key I could get into my main office and I went in and telephoned through to the house. Luckily we have a phone by the bed. Niels was totally unperturbed, his first comment being, 'Why on earth have you gone out just in my pyjama jacket and where are you phoning from?' You can imagine my comments when he eventually came down and let me in!

Andrew immediately took over the running of the laboratory with its essential work and the general health of all the donkeys and I must admit I felt the most tremendous relief on his arrival. However, his arrival has brought into perspective the fact that we really need our own hospital block here. The journey to

Exeter is really unacceptable in view of the distress it causes our donkeys and a further major project will be to design and set this up.

We are also going to set up our own scheme of inspectors so that we can more rapidly follow up the regular stream of complaints that come in from all parts of the country regarding mistreatment of donkeys. Having to rely on other societies, good though they may be, is no longer satisfactory. Donkeys have problems with which the average inspector would not normally come into contact and we really feel that they need people with specialist training to be able to assess the situation correctly. They will be trained under Andrew, and Roy Harrington has just joined us from the RSPCA to be superintendent in charge of the inspectors who will look after the donkeys' welfare throughout the country. We shall continue our non-stop work to improve the lot of the donkey in this country and abroad and to encourage our donkeys, once restored to good health themselves, to live and enjoy their lives to the full under our permanent protection.

Two poor little donkeys arrived at this time called Cilla and Alfred and their arrival was disturbing in more than one way. Cilla's owner had always deeply loved and cared for donkeys and was concerned when she began to realize Cilla was losing her eyesight. The vets were called in and seemed to think that she had a cataract starting on one eye. Despite regular treatment she eventually went blind in that eye and her owner rang us when she found Cilla was beginning to lose the sight of the other eye as well. She just couldn't bear to see her pet go blind. We collected Cilla and Alfred and brought them in and even without professional training it was apparent what was going wrong. Cilla's eyelashes were turning in and rubbing on the surface of the eye. This was causing irritation which in turn was causing the cataracts and our veterinary surgeons immediately operated to relieve the constant irritation. The sight of one eye was totally retrieved and the other improved slightly once the constant irritation was removed.

Niels and I had been invited to go to Berlin to the World Protection for Animals Conference. We hadn't been to a conference of this sort before where hundreds of delegates from all over the world and from other animal charities were to gather to discuss papers which had been produced by various experts in their own field. We were very fortunate in that we met Richard Ryder, then Chairman of the RSPCA, and Bill Jordan, who was in charge of the wildlife section of the RSPCA. They were extremely interesting people to talk to and we all got on very well indeed.

The conference itself was of immense value and we learned a great deal from the expertise of the many people we met. I gave a short talk on donkeys and found it very difficult knowing that my words were being translated into three different languages as I spoke and so many knowledgeable people were there.

The RSPCA were very interested in our purchase of Paccombe and the very beautiful woods and natural surroundings and I invited Bill Jordan to come and look round at some time in case they would like to release any small wild animals into our sanctuary area. He arranged to come and visit us at a later date.

My mother was failing fast and on the day that Bill Jordan came to see us she had a very sudden heart attack and died whilst having her cup of coffee in the kitchen. We all knew mother had cancer and didn't have very long to live and in one way it was very wonderful that she had gone so quickly and peacefully without suffering. Although I was heartbroken as usual the staff rallied round loyally and I somehow managed to keep the sanctuary running.

Now that the office had expanded and we had staff living in all the flats I was aware of a constant danger from the point of view of a serious fire. The offices were situated over a stable block and this couldn't be considered ideal from a risk point of view. I had the Health and Safety at Work officers and the fire officer round to advise us and we put in a complicated fire drill system which has almost driven us mad ever since. We have smoke and heat detectors in all the stables which sounds fine. They are supposed to set off all the fire bells when the density of smoke or the heat passes a certain level. To do its job properly the system has to be very sensitive and unfortunately the warmth emanating from a large group of donkeys is sufficient to cause a reaction. And on regular occasions anywhere between two and five a.m. all the fire bells go off and members of staff to whom we have said goodnight some hours before suddenly appear in various stages of undress. One day we hope to sort the system out but so far it seems to be eluding everybody.

After the Longleat disaster we decided we must still hold a fiesta, as it had obviously been appreciated by those attending but we decided that in 1979 we would hold it at Slade House Farm. This would alleviate the heavy cost in erecting marquees and also the trauma of the long journeys for the donkeys and staff. We chose the date of 19 August and this time the day dawned fine and bright. What a fantastic success it turned out to be. The cars streamed in from nine thirty in the morning until it closed at six at night. There were 6,000 people who came and the net result was over £3,000 raised to help the Slade Centre.

Apart from all the exhibitions on donkey welfare and their care and a tour of the Donkey Sanctuary the visitor could go into the Slade Centre where every possible type of sideshow was available and round the back of the Slade Centre the Slade donkeys were used as practical welfare demonstrations with a grooming contest and later for fancy-dress displays and a gymkhana with every donkey being led instead of ridden.

Everybody thoroughly enjoyed the day. We got outside caterers in to do the catering to prevent excess expenditure and one of the most colourful sights was the beautiful mobile fairground organ which kept the fiesta atmosphere going throughout the day. All members of the staff pulled their weight and a thoroughly good time was had by all.

John Rabjohns, one of our farm workers, affectionately known as Rabbi, made a particularly impressive sight directing the traffic in a bowler hat! I wrote a poem by way of thanks to the staff:

FIESTA 1979
A bunch of the boys were grouped round the Rover,
John giving instructions, he was main drover.
Julie was calm, her girls at the ready,
And Pat's folks were busy keeping donkeys all steady.
The helpers were there, the Centre a dream
Through which we all hoped many hundreds would stream.

184

It was only nine thirty, half an hour still to go,
When Mother was heard shouting, 'Here . . . wait a mo,
You can't go in there, it's my bit of garden.'
The large crowd turned round said, 'Begging your pardon,
We're here for Fiesta, we know we're too soon,
We wanted to come whilst there was still room.'

'All hands on deck' was the yell from above,
And everyone ran . . . t'was a labour of love.
Off went the men who were manning the gate,
Those with rosettes and programmes of the fete,
The organ arrived and Fiesta was on,
It was still very early, but ere very long,
'The traffic is queued out right to the main road,
· There's 5,000 policemen directing I'm told.'
The rumours grew stronger, but those in the Centre
Had no time to listen, it was work helter skelter.
Dot was surrounded, Tam was sold out,
Jan found her stationery almost without,
Mother found things most important to do,
She answered the questions like, 'Where is the loo?'
(Eeyore had eaten the sign with the arrow,
pointing the way down the path oh so narrow.)

Rabbi was standing in best bowler hat,
Directing the traffic and sending it back
Into the field whether it wanted or not
Parked quickly by Terry or Dave in its spot.
'Is that your celebrity, the man from McDougal?'
One visitor was heard to ask . . . very rudel!
The queue by this time stretched right down Trow Hill,
The policeman directing was feeling quite ill.

The film tent was full, with people yards thrived,
The job in the vet's was to keep worms alive
As folks in their thousands down microscopes gazed,
They learnt of our work, and were really amazed.

The Yorkes and the Gardeners, all on the go,

DBS members running a show,
Ken Birks and his family gave many a 'Shock',
And the Exmouth Equestrians ran out of stock.
Longleat was there to present the grand trophy,
Pan Books gave a super large donkey called Mokey.
Charles Judge presented a wonderful cup
For the handicapped child who had shown the most pluck.
All our young staff had plenty to do,
They collected the money, all counted by Boo.

Over five thousand attended Fiesta
(It could have been more, it could have been lesta).
Rewards in money were really quite fine,
But the best reward really was all of the time
Given so willingly in so many ways
WHOOPEE, NEXT FIESTA 364 DAYS.

There is no end to the donkeys' story; as long as there are donkeys in need, then our sanctuary will be here to help them.

Plans for the hospital have been submitted, and despite the most skilful design and use of expensive local materials so that the building is in keeping with the environment, the local council have recommended refusal to the East Devon District Council. It seems ironic that the land we wish to build on was previously a caravan site and that should we be farmers we could erect a galvanized 5,000 square foot barn with *no* permission! There is no doubt in my mind, however, that the hospital will become a reality, something so badly needed is bound to win through eventually.*

The donkeys continue to arrive in large numbers and I still learn from these delightful intelligent creatures. Spider came in a short time ago – a delightful little colt foal, but only four months

*Since this book was written, full planning permission has been received for the hospital block.

old and too young to have been separated from his mother. He was given to us by Mrs Wilkinson from the Dartmoor Livestock Protection Society who had rescued him from a Cornish market. He was so lonely on his arrival, I put in an elderly geriatric called Jennie with him for company. I had not realized the great affection that had sprung up between the two until one day I felt Spider needed a good gallop. I took them both from their special intensive care box and put them in the nursery field. Jennie stood quietly by the pond as Spider galloped about thirty yards one way, then back to see she was all right – then repeated the performance in the other direction, but on each return he pushed Jennie affectionately, pushing her nearer and nearer to the edge of the pond. I walked across and took Jennie's collar to draw her away from the edge and to my surprise dear little Spider rushed at me and did his best to deliver a kick at me in protection of his foster mother.

We have recently had reports from our new inspectorate, now at work, that conditions in one market are falling below the standards of other markets in the country, and that there were forty-eight donkeys in a knacker's yard destined for slaughter. Beach operators, whose donkeys' only food was that foraged from the council's rubbish tip, have been moved off, and a farrier has been found for a severe case of overgrown hooves in the home counties. Two donkeys were found to be unwanted and have now settled happily at the sanctuary.

It seems so sad that in this day and age there is still exploitation and cruelty to these friendly four-legged creatures, creating the need for our inspectors. In many cases it is a lack of knowledge of basic donkeys' requirements and our inspectors are always pleased to give advice to donkey-owners.

The sanctuary is now working very closely with the Donkey Breed Society and the RSPCA on the welfare side and this strengthens the position of all the charities.

At the Slade Centre trustees' last meeting it was unanimously decided that a second centre should be built. The children have really benefited so much it seems a shame to restrict it to this area. Pat Feather and I will be shortly holding an evening meeting of heads of handicapped schools and education officers in Somerset and Dorset to make sure they are as keen as we are. Although finance will cause its usual problems, we can now show people how the finished product looks and, more important, works, and I'm sure we can raise the necessary finance.

Office-wise we now have to cope with an ever-growing mail and a none-too-gradual increase in paperwork. With over 740 donkeys taken into care, every donation is needed, and despite the initial cost we have installed a computer to deal with the routine work. This means we can maintain our staff level and continue to work efficiently from our small office. Hopefully the personal touch will not be lost as so many regular donors have become very real friends and we know that to some lonely elderly people our news and letters of appreciation help to keep them going.

Although it is sad, I would like the last donkey mentioned in my book to be Pinnochio. Only recently Pinnochio, an apparently fit and healthy eight-year-old gelding, had a slight colic (pain in the stomach). The vet examined him and to his consternation found that he was having difficulty moving normally. The next day I stood watching him with dismay. I have become used to seeing over 230 handicapped children a week visit our Slade Centre and many had exactly the same symptoms Pinnochio was displaying in his stable. He seemed to have forgotten how to move his legs in order to walk, had difficulty even getting his head into his food bucket, and had no idea how to arrange his body to lie down, going in endless staggering circles, rather like a large dog, but unable to work out the mechanics of the actual movement. After three days of continuing deterioration we had no option but to put him down. We were all determined, however, to find the cause of this terrible affliction he had received so suddenly. The vet arranged for his brain to go to a top veterinary neurologist in Cambridge, but during the post-mortem was astounded to find the donkey had died from a broken neck. He estimated from the round edges of the fracture that the actual break had occurred very early in life and the pain of the colic and a sudden neck movement had displaced the vertebrae broken several years ago, giving the distressing symptoms.

We were all deeply upset, but one night some time later I found myself wide awake, comparing his actions with those of the handicapped children. How many of these children, with in-explicable handicaps, had had a neck x-ray in case a similar injury had caused their symptoms? Could it be that during birth, particularly in emergency deliveries, the head had been forcibly turned to ease the shoulders out, injuring the neck? Many of the Slade children hold their heads at a strange angle – could it be neck damage? All these thoughts have been passed on to the medical profession; it would be wonderful if a little donkey called Pinnochio could help explain the plight of even *one* stricken child.

We have many critics, those who feel the money we spend on donkeys could be better spent on old people, on young people, on battered babies – the list is endless, all worthy causes, but my love is donkeys and it is to them I wish my efforts to go. To me they are the most beautiful, the most underrated, animals in the world – and as long as they need my help they shall have it.

Bestselling Fiction and Non-Fiction

☐	**Modesty Blaise**	Peter O'Donnell	95p
☐	**Falconhurst Fancy**	Kyle Onstott	£1.50p
☐	**The Pan Book of Card Games**	Hubert Phillips	£1.25p
☐	**The New Small Garden**	C. E. Lucas Phillips	£2.50p
☐	**Fools Die**	Mario Puzo	£1.50p
☐	**Everything Your Doctor Would Tell You If He Had the Time**	Claire Rayner	£4.95p
☐	**Polonaise**	Piers Paul Read	95p
☐	**The 65th Tape**	Frank Ross	£1.25p
☐	**Nightwork**	Irwin Shaw	£1.25p
☐	**Bloodline**	Sidney Sheldon	95p
☐	**A Town Like Alice**	Nevil Shute	£1.25p
☐	**Lifeboat VC**	Ian Skidmore	£1.00p
☐	**Just Off the Motorway**	John Slater	£1.95p
☐	**Wild Justice**	Wilbur Smith	£1.50p
☐	**The Spoiled Earth**	Jessica Stirling	£1.75p
☐	**That Old Gang of Mine**	Leslie Thomas	£1.25p
☐	**Caldo Largo**	Earl Thompson	£1.50p
☐	**Future Shock**	Alvin Toffler	£1.95p
☐	**The Visual Dictionary of Sex**	Eric J. Trimmer	£5.95p
☐	**The Flier's Handbook**		£4.95p

All these books are available at your local bookshop or newsagent, or can be ordered direct from the publisher. Indicate the number of copies required and fill in the form below

Name _____
(block letters please)

Address _____

_____

Send to Pan Books (CS Department), Cavaye Place, London SW10 9PG
Please enclose remittance to the value of the cover price plus:

25p for the first book plus 10p per copy for each additional book ordered to a maximum charge of £1.05 to cover postage and packing
Applicable only in the UK

While every effort is made to keep prices low, it is sometimes necessary to increase prices at short notice. Pan Books reserve the right to show on covers and charge new retail prices which may differ from those advertised in the text or elsewhere